T0077676

The Power of
the Gift

Larry Matthews

iUniverse, Inc.
New York   Bloomington

The Power of the Gift

iUniverse books may be ordered through booksellers or by contacting:

*iUniverse
1663 Liberty Drive
Bloomington, IN 47403
www.iuniverse.com
1-800-Authors (1-800-288-4677)*

*Because of the dynamic nature of the Internet, any Web addresses or
links contained in this book may have changed since publication and may
no longer be valid.*

*ISBN: 978-1-4502-0436-1 (sc)
ISBN: 978-1-4502-0437-8 (ebk)*

Library of Congress Control Number: 2009914222

Printed in the United States of America

iUniverse rev. date: 02/03/2010

THE POWER
OF THE
GIFT

This easy to read book "The Power of The Gift", is designed to help you change your life with cut through the chase answers to questions which have been preventing your success.

If you are looking for answers that will lead you to a life of prosperity, good health and happiness, then this is the book you have been waiting for.

In understanding the power of the gift, you will gain wisdom, understanding and knowledge: true keys to a life of success.

Brace yourself, you are about to begin
a journey into a kingdom that was there
all the time and most of all, you are
royalty in that kingdom.

LARRY
MATTHEWS

ACKNOWLEDGEMENTS

To Your Highness, thank you for saving me from me. I am eternally grateful, thank You so much.

To my wonderful mother, Mary Bozeman who never gave up hope that her son would one day be returned to her. Your love keeps my heart in remembrance. Whether I was right or wrong, you were always there, extending the love that only a mother could know and show. Your example and encouragement are priceless, I love you very much.

To my father Eugene Bozeman who has always been a great father, not to mention provider for our family. Your love for each of your six children is just as unwavering now as it was in the beginning. You have always been there to support me when I tried to do what was right. Even now, you continue to work in being a guiding light, showing us how we should walk on the planet, with much love and respect.

To my brothers and sister, André, Stanley, Gina and Dana, I wrote this book as a gift of my talents to the world. I also did it to set the pace for a new day, where we always strive to do the right things for the right reason, always setting the example of being the bigger person, it's called character. I love all of you very, very, much. Stay focused, you know who comes First.

To my sister Deidre Brewster, You were there when we all needed you most. Fortunately, for us that is all the time.

You have truly been a strong example of what love looks like while here on planet Earth and I think it is safe to say that I am not alone. Thank you very much sis, I love you very much.

To my grandparents, Sinclair Bozeman and (Rosa May Bozeman **in memoriam)**, thank you for being an inspiration in my life. I have had the honor of calling myself your grandson and I will try to live up to the title the best I can. I will always love you.

To my grandmother Lillian Lawson, thank you so much for being one of my first teachers. It was you who told me to **think about the other fellow** all those times when I thought it was all about me. Your love and guidance can be found in some of the chapters of this book. I love you very much, thanks.

To all of my nieces and nephews, I am trying to set an example. I wrote this book with you in mind. I have endeavored to provide information which will serve you well in your lives. I only ask that you read it. Who knows, maybe you will try to write something too? I love all of you very much. La Shawn, La Quan, Ashley Matthews, Tiffany Bozeman. Diana Brewster, Maketa Rosa Bozeman, Tamaz and Tamia Bozeman.

To my aunt Ava, Vernell Matthews, I love you very much. We have always been close. I can always talk to you and come clean. Thank you for your inspiration; you were always a fair person, One Love.

To Uncle (Lynn) Lindsey Barrett **in memoriam,** thank you for your love in the early years of my life. I'm trying.

To "daddy" (Willis Moore **in memoriam),** I remember, thank you for your great example of making the best out of the hand you were dealt. To   Beatrice and Sara great sister in laws I love you both.

To Penny Henderson, you have done a tremendous job in transcribing my gibberish hand writing. Your untiring efforts are well appreciated Thank you.

To Ms. Lorraine Darling, I really appreciated your editing assistance and all of the friendly suggestions you inserted for me to consider. Thank you very much.

To one of my dearest friends on the planet; Mr. Terran Mosley., I am forever grateful for the friendship you have showed me over the years. You have always believed in me, even when I didn't believe in myself. You never judged but always loved me the feeling is mutual. Thank you.

To Mr. John Gibson and Mr. Eric Heath Williams thank both of you for your unwavering support. I need your services and you did not let me down, with much respect. One.

And to all those people who have helped me along the way, although I have not mentioned your name, you are not forgotten. Thank you.

Power of the Gift

Offers.

A clear easy to understand explanation, why our thoughts are powerful and creative, and how we can use this power, to change our lives.

INTRODUCTION

A personal letter

Dear Brothers and Sisters:

I hardly know where to start. How did things get so far? I can remember a time when people cared.

A time where we didn't have a whole lot of material things, but, we had a whole lot of love. Today, each and every day, I witness all kinds of crazy things. Among those things are, teenage killings, lack of interest in education, disrespect for ourselves and others. And all of those negative behaviors, we so readily cling to. It saddens me greatly to see so many people just throw away this precious gift we call life.

And for whatever the reason may be, hope for many, does not exist. Many times it is not their fault.

They simply have not found the answers they are looking for that will help to give them direction in having a life that, they believe is worth living.

It is for this very reason; I am compelled to write this book. It is my deepest desire that the writings contained in its pages will help you find at least some of the answers you are looking for. In this book, you will find information that has the power to transform you, and change your life.

I believe every person on the planet should try to be a guiding light of hope and inspiration for their brothers and sisters. I know we can do better than we are doing.

I set before you a few suggested goals which I believe are worth striving for in making our world a better place. I believe each person is going to have to find their purpose in life. Once you have found your purpose, you have to pursue it with all of your heart, soul and might. We are going to have to learn to let our individual lights shine in everything we set out to do. Whether we are in the classroom, on the basketball court or wherever we are, we are going to have to put our heart in everything we do. Do it, with all of your might.

We have to pursue all of our endeavors as though our very lives depended on it, and at this point, from what I am seeing every day, our lives do depend on it.

We are going to have to view our fellow humans as our brothers and sisters. We have to come into a conscious awareness that we really are more alike than different. We are all striving for similar basic needs and a sense of well being. We are going to have to truly want for our brothers what we want for ourselves. But just wanting will not be enough; we are going to have to learn to serve our communities, starting at home with our own families. We have to understand that as long as there is despair and confusion in the lives of our brothers, we cannot be at peace. We are going to have to learn the fact that, we really are our brother's keeper. Now you may say, I understand what you are saying, but why should I make a conscious effort to help out where I can? In response to that, I would say help out, because it is time for a change, and change is exactly what we need in America. We have to rid ourselves of the old **business as usual** attitudes we were taught, and have followed for far too long. **What we need is a REVOLUTION**.

Yes, that's right, a revolution. Not a revolution in the sense of physical destructive actions. No, what we need is **a revolution of individual action**. We need a revolution where people began to break away from "that's just the way things are", and start to trust their own creative self. We need a revolution where people stop following the beaten path, but instead, make a path and leave a trail for others to follow.

We have to make a conscious effort to change our homes, neighborhoods, cities and even the nation. We have to abandon the idea of going with the flow just because people say, "that's the way it is". We have to learn to stand up without being afraid.

We have to make the most out of this experience we call life. We are not going to be here forever. Therefore, we have to do something worthwhile, which will help to make the world a better place.

I believe we need education, wisdom, understanding and a strong desire to be the best person we can be while we walk on this planet, is the first step to a new beginning. It is time that we take our place in society as decent people, and not just some of us, but all of us.

Decent, such a simple word, yet it carries a whole lot of meaning. To be called a decent man, woman, boy or girl is a title worth striving for. I believe in change because I too looked for answers for a long time and now those answers which I looked for and found are working for me. They are helping me transform into a better person. In this book, I have endeavored to share with you what I have learned about being made in the image of God, and the power that, that gift carries.

The knowledge and use of the gift we possess, has literally elevated my life to joy, happiness and prosperity. I pray that it will work for you as well. It is through this new found awareness that, I have made a commitment in this life to strive to do what I believe to be right, simply because it is right. It is through this awareness, that I long to see the day when we value each other, family and education over all those material things that seem to have thrown us off track. With a humble heart, we have to return to our creator. I am certain; He will welcome us with open arms. It is a fine gesture when we kneel and pray in our houses of worship but, I believe that we have to do more than just kneeling and praying, I believe we have to learn to walk with God each and every day, much like a friend and companion . But our first step has to be coming into the knowledge of the truth. The truth is that we were born to be sons and daughters of the living God**. We were sent here to help, not hurt each other.** It is high time that we, members of the human race, grow-up. We have to take responsibility for our own lives and the lives that we helped to bring into the world. God knows our abilities, now we have to know them. It is in knowing our abilities that it is possible for us to have life and have it abundantly.

I sincerely pray that this book will serve you well. However, I am simply planting the seeds and God will do the increase.

With great love and respect

Bro. Larry

P.S. I am writing this letter to all of my brothers and sisters ,Red, Yellow, Black and White, it is intended for you.

Table of Contents

CHAPTER # 1

There are admirable potentialities in every human being. Believe in your strength…….. Learn to repeat endlessly to yourself, '<u>It all depends on me.</u>"
Andre Gide

<u>In search of Happiness</u>

Who does not want to be happy? There isn't one person on the planet who is striving for a life of misery, pain and suffering. Of course not: a person would not be normal unless he wanted to experience a life of joy and happiness; it is our Nature and Natural instinct to seek happiness.   And what is happiness? Well, for the most part, happiness involves being safe, having enough food, financial security, good health and a meaningful relationship. We all can agree, if we had these things just the way we wanted them, we would be "**happy**".

However, for most people, happiness is usually a few moments here and there but rarely lasting.

<u>A question that always puzzled me was: Why are some people better off financially, have better health, and just overall happier lives than others?</u>   These questions haunted me for years, especially in times when I was financially broke or depressed.

Finally, I came to the conclusion that these people were no different than me. The only difference was in the way they thought. When I realized that the only difference between them and me was the way we thought, **I decided, I needed to change my thinking**. Re-evaluate how I looked at life and the things around me. But if I was going to change my thinking, what was I supposed to be thinking about that would bring joy and happiness. The one thing I did understand was that, just as no one could live for me, no one could think for me. I would have to think for myself. Basically, all I wanted to know was their secret.

MY LIFE WAS A WRECK

Looking back, I clearly remember my life at that moment. **I wanted a better life for myself but was not sure how to go about getting it;** I noticed that most people in my neighborhood were just like me, **barely existing.** Many of them lived every day of their lives doing the same old routines. They dreamed all day without ever taking any action. They ran the streets, or spent most of their time in front of the T.V., as if life was forever. Like me, some were victims of substance abuse. The choice of drugs was usually heroin, cocaine or beer. Many of the younger ones either followed a street gang or were victimized by one. This would continue until they either met with an early grave or eventually grew old, usually before their time and died.

I did not want to continue living like this. I wanted to rise above the neighborhood madness and confusion. I wanted good health. I wanted financial security. In short, I wanted to be successful and I wanted to be happy.

IN RETROSPECT.

My personal history is that, I was born in Detroit Michigan and had lived in the south until I was nine years old. It was through my actions of stealing sodas from the local service station that caused my family to be evicted from our one room apartment. Left with no other alternative, it was decided that my father would stay behind while my mother along with the children travel north, to Long Island, N.Y., to live with my aunt Ella and her family. We arrived in the summer of 1968 and shortly thereafter my father joined us. He was a hard working man, who believed his first responsibility was to provide for the family. In fact, both mom and dad were loving parents. They worked day and night. I was the oldest of six children and the responsibility of caring for my younger siblings rested with me. The year was 1975 and I was now in high school. I was a fairly bright student. I always maintained good grades, but somehow never felt comfortable in my own skin. I always felt less than other children. In 1975 drugs were rapidly becoming a fact of life in the community. As a result, drug awareness classes were offered in our schools. We were encouraged to have open conversations with our parents about the apparent drug invasion and the possible dangers involved. I remember being curious as hell about drugs and on a number of occasions, I asked my mother if we could have family discussions about drug abuse. She responded with a firm "no" and her reason was that she was not interested in the subject of drug abuse and as a result, felt no need to engage in that sort of conversation with us. Although she had no interest in the subject, my interest did not lessen.

The following year 1976, I was a high school senior and soon would have the experience of the senior prom. On prom night, I was introduced to my first marijuana joint. The feeling and experience were magical. I wanted that night to last forever. After high school, I attended Jersey City University, located in Jersey City N.J., where I received a Bachelor of Science degree in Accounting; I was twenty three years old at the time. My involvement, use and ultimate addiction to heroin and cocaine began in my college years and lasted over two decades after graduation. It was because of my addition to drugs that I experienced the county jail. By the time I was thirty years old, my life was all downhill. Drug abuse had reduced me from an educated professional accountant, to the life of a lying scam artist. When I was not scamming, I could usually be found in the neighborhood pan handling for change. There was even a point in my life where I became homeless, often sleeping at local shelters or abandoned buildings. And because I could not be trusted, my parents would not allow me to stay the night at their home, for fear they would wake to find their valuables missing. This kind of meaningless existence lasted for over twenty years. During those years, there were many times when my parents tried their best to talk sense into my head. Sometimes, I could see pain, hurt and disappointment in their eyes. They wanted a better life for me. But I could not see the logic. To me, my life of addiction all made sense, when in reality, year after year, I continued to dig a deeper and deeper hole for myself. It was only after I became spiritually bankrupt, with no alternatives left, that I came to the conclusion that I was defeated. It was as though one day I woke up and realized that I no longer wanted to play the drug game. However, even though I no longer wanted to play the drug game, as far as the drugs were concerned, they were in charge and the game was far from over. I had long learned that any action repeated over and over again, soon becomes a habit. And as far as I was concerned, drugs were definitely on the top of that list. Anyone who has ever been addicted to narcotics will tell you that, you don't just stop. If you have used drugs for any substantial amount of time and decide to quit, then brace yourself because, you are about to be in the fight of your life. It was no different for me. The day I decided to stop using drugs was the day I learned what it meant to fight for your life. It was in my attempt to recover from my addiction that I first begin to gain a conscious awareness of the power of the gift we possess. My sincere prayers, along with a strong desire to stop using drugs, led me to the East Orange Veterans Hospital, where I sought help. I had been there many times in the past but only as a means to get some temporary relief. In previous times, I had no intention of stopping my drug abuse and strangely, whenever I came, they never had a bed available for a new patient. This time it was different. I was now committed to stopping and I wanted my life to change. I remember checking in at the registration desk and was told that I would have to see a counselor in building 18, who would access my condition. When I arrived at building 18, I was seen right away. The counselor's name was Mary. She started by asking me to explain exactly what my problem was. I told her that I had been addicted to heroin and cocaine for more than twenty years and that I was tired, scared and lonely. I wanted to be free from addiction and I could not do it alone. I needed help. I asked her were there any open beds available and if so, would it be possible for me to be admitted on that day. She explained that there were beds available but because of my heroin addiction, I would first have to go to a detox facility before being admitted. She immediately began to make phone calls to local detox centers and surprisingly, the first call she made, they accepted me.

When I realized that things were moving in my favor, I started to feel full inside and I wanted to cry but I did not. Somehow I felt that God had really heard my prayers this time. And as a result, He was making moves behind the scenes designed to help me. The counselor explained that immediately after my detox treatment there would be a bed waiting for me. With those words came relief and hope, it was as if the weight of the world had been lifted from my shoulders. Now, I could not help it. I broke down and started crying uncontrollably. I tried to maintain my composure but I could not. Inside, I felt nothing but pain. She tried to console me. She assured me that everything would work out for me and that I was now moving in the direction of a new life. What she did not understand was; I was crying because, although I wanted the pain to stop, deep down I knew there existed the possibility that I might not recover and that very thought frightened me beyond hope. But, in the mist of it all, I could feel a power greater than myself helping me. How many times in the past had I attempted to be admitted into this very facility? Only to be told that there were no open beds and the waiting list was long. Now that I was serious about my recovery, it appeared that God was showing me that He would be there for me. I could feel His presence.

Detox went well. Immediately after detox, I returned to the facility in East Orange, N.J., which, lasted for thirty days. Afterwards, I was sent to a veteran's inpatient facility in Bath, New York. It was during my stay at Bath, New York that I realized without a shadow of a doubt that I was fighting for my life. My greatest battles usually occurred in my dreams while I slept. Although, I wanted to stop using and depending on drugs, every night for the first thirty nights or more, I would have dreams that always involved using drugs. During the day, I would consciously denounce the use of drugs and every night the drug dreams would re- appear. I would wake up sweating and frightened with the thought that, I was not ever going to recover. I needed strength, inner strength but, where would it come from? Every night I played spades with my fellow vet brothers. I would usually be the first person to leave the card table, claiming that I wanted to take an early shower and prepare for the next day. I would leave them smiling as though everything was fine. When in reality, it was not. Little did they know, when I reached the shower, where I knew no one was watching, I would begin to cry and pray, asking God to help me. I cannot remember taking too many showers where I did not find myself crying out for help. My greatest fear was that the drug dreams were an indication of how I really felt about using drugs.

I thought the dreams meant, I still wanted to get high. I had to devise a strategy. I realized that if I was going to win this fight, I would need to get the upper hand. Therefore, I sought wisdom and understanding. For me losing was not an option. I was determined to recover. The crazy thing about wisdom and understanding was that, I was not exactly sure what it was. I did remember hearing in Sunday school that King Solomon of Israel did not ask for riches, but instead he asked for wisdom and understanding to lead the people. And it was no secret that I needed to be lead to a life free from addiction. It was in my search for wisdom and understanding that I stumbled on the **Science of Mind**, which outlined the spiritual power humans, possess to change their lives. And because I was desperate, this was welcomed information. I decided to give it a try. Every night for four months, I would read books on the power we possess through the use of our minds and how we could use this power to effectively shape our future. Each day I searched the internet and library for books on the subject of the science of mind. I discovered, Thomas Troward author of "the Hidden Power "and Ernest Holmes the author of "The Science of Mind" They both offered information which gave me confidence, strength and hope, that I possessed the ability to change my life for the better.

The more I read and studied, the more I tried to apply the concepts to my life. And although, I was a firm believer in the gospel of Jesus Christ, I found no conflict of interest in my religious beliefs and the Science of Mind, especially since they both agreed that a man is transformed by the renewing of his mind. After two months of applying the concepts of mind to my life, the drug dreams ceased. My inpatient process lasted well over six months. And within that time, I became thoroughly entrenched in the works of these Science of Mind authors. Upon my release, I returned to New Jersey but did not inform my family. I did not inform them because; I was learning to depend on God for my needs. I also felt that this would be another opportunity to try out my new found knowledge. Moreover, I also realized that I was fresh in my recovery and I should therefore make a conscious effort to follow the suggestions given to me by my therapist and counselors. I had saved money through a work program and used it to secure a small room for myself at the local YMCA.

I also used my savings to look for a job. I bought into the idea of the power we possess inside of us, which can be used to shape our lives and as a result, decided that, I would contact my family only after I had secured a job. I was certain, I would find a job. I knew I was trying to live life better and as a result, I believed God would help me in my efforts. I had not worked on a traditional job in over twenty years. But none the less, I was certain that I would get a job and I did. After seven days of searching, I landed a job. You cannot begin to imagine the feelings of joy and confidence I was now experiencing. After twenty years, there would finally be a paycheck with my name on it. I also attended regular NA meetings and followed their simple suggestions. Gradually, I could see signs that my life was changing for the better. Things were looking up. I now began to see life with new eyes, you might say, I was born again. Through my belief in the concept of being made in the image of God and the possibilities that came with it, I began to feel that the sky was the limit. Through the grace of God I had beaten the odds. My only challenge now was finding the truth and wisdom, needed to bring a lasting change into my life. I had tasted freedom from addiction and now, I wanted to taste a life of happiness and prosperity.

In my search for happiness and prosperity, I remembered a piece of literature I had read in the past, written by a man named James T. Allen – entitled " As a man thinketh"- Mr. Allen's work had been crowned one of the most inspirational pieces of all time. The focus of his writing dealt with the power of a man's mind to create heaven or hell right here on Earth. He claimed that "man is made or unmade by himself. In the armory of thought, he forges the weapons by which he destroys himself. He also fashions the tools with which he builds for himself heavenly mansions of joy, strength and peace".

James T. Allen's writings suggested that the way people use their minds to think, played an important role in the quality of life they lived.

His writing got my attention. I became interested. **As I continued my study of the Science of Mind, I realized for the first time in my life that, I finally found something that actually made sense to me.** The Science of Mind, not only made sense to me, but it was something so practical that I found no difficulty in applying the concepts and principles to my life.

And since this book is entitled **the "Power of the Gift", I will start by discussing how to activate the gift we possess inside to change our lives.**

I believe if a person applies these principles on a consistent basis, <u>whatever goal he places before</u> <u>him will be realized</u>. It is just a matter of time, patience and consistency. **Success will come.**

The study of mind is established on the premises that all we see, say, think or do, is always a thought first. Just take a moment to look around you, every piece of furniture, every building, automobile or the clothes you are wearing, were first a thought in a person's mind. When we come into a conscious awareness of this knowledge, we gain strength and power. **<u>This is the law of thought, which states that everything is a thought before becoming a reality.</u>** Thinking always comes before the action. James T. Allen says that "Act is the blossom of thought and joy and suffering are its fruit"

Now, when we study the power of our thoughts, we are studying the Science of Mind. Like any other science it is exact. Meaning, it is based on the premise that, if you do this, then you will get this-but if you do that then, you will get that.

If you remember earlier, I said that it puzzled me why some people were more successful than others and that I wanted to know their secret. <u>I now know their secret.</u> <u>They were using the Science of Mind</u>. They learned the art of thinking in a way that brings their desires into their lives. They learned how to activate the power within themselves and therewith think prosperity into their lives.

And since I have found the principles of the Science of mind to be of great value, I would like to share them with you. I only ask that you keep an open mind and see how much sense they make.

The first time I heard "**As a man thinketh in his heart so is he**" I was in church. I heard it and it meant absolutely nothing to me. The reason I didn't understand how important that one little phrase meant was because I did not have a complete knowledge of "myself". I don't mean myself in terms of my family heritage. I mean myself in a much greater sense. I mean my divine self. In religious circles, it is common knowledge, that man was made in the image of God and for a long time, I thought it meant that a man, not a woman, somehow had the image of God.

I had no idea that God was an equal opportunity employer. Men and women are both made in the image of God. They both possess the power of the gift.

Today, I have a greater understanding of being made in the image of God and how it ties into "**As a man thinketh**". To understand what is meant by being made in the image of God, I had to get some understanding of the nature of God.

I started by looking at world religions. Christianity, Islam, Judaism and Hinduism, they all have their personal beliefs concerning God. And although they differ on many things, one belief I found they have in common is that they all believe that God is a spirit and has no physical form. They further believe that humans are made in His image. And since humans possess a physical body, being made in the image of God has to mean that some part of humans must be spirit.

They also claim that **He is a creator, our Creator, and the first cause of our existence**. Now whatever qualities and characteristics He possesses since we are made in His image, then we too must possess the same. But to make the comparison of the spirit of God and man, I recall on one occasion reading the analogy like this; "If you could compare the entire ocean to the spirit of God, the ocean representing His spirit and you took a teaspoon of water from the ocean, the water from the ocean and the water in the teaspoon would be the same, the only difference would be in the quantity, not the quality, so what the ocean could do-which represents the power and spirit of God, the teaspoon of water could also do, just on a smaller scale. Now imagine that teaspoon of His spirit being poured into us". What exactly would that mean? Well what it would mean is that every person walking on the planet has God's power inside of them which would include the power to create. It would mean that the title Creator-which applies to God on the large scale, would also apply to you and me on a smaller scale.

This is the beginning of the truth about who we really are. The great teacher said "**you shall know the truth and the truth shall make you free**", for me, this was the beginning of one of those truths that would make me free.

What I want you to understand is this: **we all have a divine inheritance which is that teaspoon of spirit from God;** it is the life force which causes us to live, move and have our being. So we can start by saying that spirit is the only creative force in the universe. Spirit always existed and always will exist. There is a part of this spirit inside of us. It loves us, because It not only created us but It also resides in us.

No one could ask for a greater love than this and no greater love could be given. We can now conclude that one of the characteristics of spirit is that it is a creative force.

Creativity is Its nature and It cannot stop its nature to create. And since we have a part of the Creator inside of us, we cannot get around the fact that we too are creators, whether intentional or not, we are constantly creating. It is through the ***Science of Mind that we get a logical understanding of our creative nature***.

Science of Mind states that "**the first step in our creative process is through the power of our thinking**". It says that "A man is literally what he thinks, his character being the complete sum of his thoughts". **At every turn in our lives, we are what we think.**

Everything we accomplish or fail to accomplish in our lives is a direct result of our thoughts.

Thoughts produce a creative vibration which possesses the power to set energy in motion. This energy, once set in motion, has the power to create positive or negative conditions in our lives. Many times we have heard **we reap what we sow or what goes around comes around**. Now with our thinking this could not be truer. The vibrations we send from our minds are real. One example I like to give has to do with meeting people. Many times you meet people and right away you say" I don't like the vibes I'm getting from that person" or "I like their vibes". On the one hand, "I don't like the vibes" can be explained by the fact that the energy you are receiving from that person does not match your energy level. This has been known to give us a feeling of uneasiness. It usually suggests that these two people have different agendas.

Whereas on the other hand, when you meet someone and you receive their energy level in a positive way, you have been known to say "I like the vibes I get from that person". The truth is that the energy vibration is a match and therefore welcomed.

It is this energy vibration we use through the power of our mind that creates anything we may need or desire to bring into our reality.

When you change your thinking, you will change your life.

I hope you are beginning to understand yourself a little better now; therefore, I would like to look a little deeper into the power of thought. You see, most people are running around every day and for the most part they go to bed every night and cannot clearly say that they have accomplished anything worthwhile for that day. They would probably make better use of their time if they truly understood the law of their being. To be idle is against our nature. It creates depression. We were born to be creators; it is our nature to create. What people do not understand is that our thoughts connect us to the power of eternal spirit, **it is our divine inheritance.**

And, although I was not aware of it, the first time I witnessed the power we possess inside of us, I was in the fourth grade. The situation was that my fourth grade class had gone on a class trip to Coney Island New York. I will never forget it because this was the first time that my mother had given me a dollar bill. In those days money was tight and children in my family were never given anything more than a quarter. As a result of the school sending a notice home that the class would have lunch at the then famous Nathan's Hot

Dog Stand in Coney Island N.Y.,, my mother decided to gave me a dollar. The dollar I received was to be used for my lunch money. In those days you could by a soda and a hot dog for about ninety cents. Our class trip was in the month of April and the weather was still a little chilly. As a result, we walked along the beach but did not take our shoes off. I had a constant fear of losing my dollar; I checked my pocket regularly to ensure that I still had it. However, when the time came to purchase my food, I reached for the dollar and it was not there.

My fear of losing the dollar had become a reality. I panicked. And as a result, when my teacher looked away, I dashed off to the beach to look for my dollar. I soon discovered that the sea shore was larger than I remembered. I also noticed that there were numerous steps leading from the boardwalk to the beach. I could not be certain where we were or where I should begin looking. I became discouraged and began to cry. At that point, I remembered my grandmother saying "ask God, He could do anything". So with my eyes closed and crying, I began to say repeatedly "Lord God, please return my dollar". "Lord God, please return my dollar". I believed. I believed with the faith of a fourth grader who did not know enough to doubt. Amazingly, when I opened my eyes, the wind was blowing a dollar bill to my feet. The sight of the dollar produced unspeakable joy. And although I was relieved, I had no idea that I was in fact using the power of the gift. The God nature we possess. In retrospect, when I analyze the situation, I realize that because I entertained fearful thoughts of losing the dollar, my concentrated thoughts made it come true. Today, I understand that whatever we focus our thoughts on with intense concentration, will begin to activate our inner power to make it a reality. This was further proved, when in desperation, I began to have faith in the power of

God;I was again without conscious knowledge, unleashing the God power I possessed to bring the dollar back to me. The intense feelings and beliefs of a fourth grader made the situation a reality in both instances. It is through the Science of Mind that I understand what took place. And more importantly, it all makes perfectly good sense.

King Solomon says in the bible's book of Proverbs "If wisdom is the principle thing then get wisdom and in all thy getting get understanding".

Understanding becomes knowledge only when it is applied to our lives. The great thing about getting this knowledge is that from it, we begin to understand that we can consciously change our lives through our thinking. It is when we decide to make a commitment to do anything worthwhile, that our creative energies are activated, which will began to help us. This is why it is called the power of the gift. It is through the power of the gift we possess inside, that we receive salvation. **And salvation is defined as "to be delivered from difficulty or evil"**. It is through the activation of this power that, we receive all the guidance we need to succeed in whatever we set out to do.

 Our thought process is powerful; it creates our present reality which in turn will become our future. One of the great mistakes people make and especially our youth, is in the misguided notion that their future is going to be great when they reach a certain age, a professional basketball player, a famous rapper or some other individual of importance. What they fail to realize is this: the future is not a place where they are headed and when they get there everything will be laid-out for them—just placed in their lap. The truth is that every individual walking on planet Earth makes their future by the choices that they make today. Wise choices today pave the way for a better tomorrow, there is no other way. It is the only way. When we can appreciate the fact that our thinking today makes our future tomorrow, we get a clear understanding how it is that "**We reap what we sow**".

Subsequent to these laws, if we do not make healthy productive choices, we are heading down a road of destruction. Now here's the thing and there's no getting around this –man's thought- energy operates within the **law of attraction,** and the law of attraction says like attracts like.

In simple, terms, the law of attraction can be explained like this, if you feel and think a particular way, then by virtue of your creative nature, the law of attraction gives you more of the same feelings. This will show up as conditions in our lives. The law of attraction is actually a law of nature that is activated by the vibrations we generate from our thoughts.

Therefore, when we constantly think negative, destructive thoughts which are fueled by feelings of hatred, anger, worry, doubt, fear, envy, or jealousy, the energy produced from these thoughts are sent out into the universal energy field which sends more of those same feelings back to us. And as a result, these thoughts create negative, non productive episodes in our lives.

Happiness is everyone's desire. And no one in their right mind can honestly say that they are happy when they experience feelings of fear, doubt, hatred, anger, jealously or being judgmental.

When we experience negative feelings, we are not expressing love, nor are we at peace.

Negative thoughts and feelings take our energy level from a high positive, productive state, to a low, negative, non-productive state. This in turn produces stress, which disrupts our peace and steals our joy. <u>Peace is our natural state,</u> and when we allow our peace to be disrupted; we block the flow of positive energy we would otherwise receive. People should be aware of the fact that when you block the positive flow of energy, you limit your inner strength, and inspiration. This is one of the reasons why many people cannot cope with the everyday challenges of life; they do not possess inner strength due to a poor flow of spiritual energy. In their negative thinking they think they are doing harm to others when all along they are harming themselves.

It is also worth mentioning that people, who habitually entertain negative thoughts over a period of time, are more likely to suffer poor physical health.

Their sufferings stem from negative energy mentally generated. Negative energies create physical imbalance, which in turn promotes high blood pressure, diabetes, chronic depression and heart disease. When we have inner peace, we are better able to overcome any challenge that may stand in the way of our goals.

Moreover, as you might imagine, since negative thoughts produce disharmony and creates negative non-productive realities, the very opposite thoughts produce a state of inner peace and harmony, thereby creating a positive, prosperous and healthy reality. These thoughts and feelings are joy, love, hope, beauty, faith, courage, being non judgmental, having acceptance, gratitude, thanksgiving, appreciation and fair play.

These are feelings that send vibrations from our inner being that promote life and expand our positive life experiences. With these feelings, we experience peace because; they are aligned with our true nature. When we engage in these positive feelings, we are telling the law of attraction this is what we want to experience more of. As a result, the law of attraction brings more of the same into our lives, which returns to us in the form of good physical and mental health, prosperity and happiness.

It seems to me that once a person gets knowledge of the power of his thought energies and understands how they work, then and only then can he intelligently begin to make the life he dreams of having.

It's all about our thinking.

Now as you look around, you will see people dealing with many different things in their lives. Basically people are looking for answers that will guide them to happiness and prosperity. And this is accomplished by using the power of our minds**. Humans' posses the power to think and thinking is where creation starts. I cannot emphasize this enough.**

We live in a world of mind represented by physical manifestation and human actions.

And when I look and consider the idea that everything I see was a thought before it was a reality, I can only agree because these things could not have come any other way, except that, they were first thought of by some person using the power of their mind.   When we embrace the power of the gift we possess, we become confident that we too can change our lives for the better.

We all have the power to think and therefore create our own reality.   We are not bound by present conditions or circumstances.   We are all creators, it is our birthright. By our very nature, we are constantly using the law of our being, whether we are aware of it or not. **And although we are all creators, many people never intelligently tap into their ability to create a life of success.**

They live their entire lives and never come to the knowledge of the truth of who they really are and the power they possess, which is a gift from the father of light.

The apostle Paul says in 2 Tim. 3-7 That people are "ever learning but never coming to the knowledge of the truth"

They live from day to day, and whatever life deals them, they accept.   They are people who live in a great ocean of infinite possibilities where things would be different for them if they would only make intelligent choices.   Instead, they do not. They exist in a go- with- the- flow- attitude.

They are constantly looking at other people who have achieved success and say Wow!!!   Tragically they are not consciously aware that they too possess the ability to be great. They do not understand that greatness also lies within them.

Instead they choose to live a life of excuses

It is a fact that we were all born into situations and conditions where we had no say in the matter.

We were not all born into a loving family, with money, no problems and no family issues.

Almost all of us, without exception, came into this world facing some challenge. The world is also full of people who decided to take a stand in their lives. They made the choice to meet the challenge to rise above whatever hand life had dealt them. They realized that the change they needed in their lives would have to be made by them.

You are no different. They had to do it for themselves and so will you if you are going to have the life you are dreaming of. The one thing these people did was this; they simply made a choice to dream of living a different life. They went a step farther and followed their dreams.

They made the choice to be an individual and as an individual they took a stand and said;

Although I cannot judge you- that is what you are doing and this is what I choose to do, because this is what makes the most sense to me. When you exercise your right to be an individual, there are inner signals that will help you make the choices that are right for you.

I have found that whenever I feel uncomfortable on the inside, that's usually my inner self letting me know that I am going in the wrong direction.

It is the individual, not the follower, who dares to dream of a better life and makes the commitment to follow that dream by taking action, thereby making the dream a reality.

No one can ever achieve a life of happiness, prosperity and health by following what I call a "mob mentality". When you follow a "mobs mentality" you are giving your thought energies over to a control that is a lie. It is not you.

 To blindly follow anyone when it makes no sense to you is the act of a coward.

You cannot express your greatness by being a coward. – You are an original and unique expression of the Creator. Accept and appreciate it.

When you give up your individuality by going with the flow of what everyone else is doing, you are showing a lack of appreciation of the special talents and gifts you possess. How will you ever come into your greatness without first having an appreciation of the unique and original qualities you possess.   You were made the way you are for a reason.

We have to learn to be thankful for our own unique and original qualities and make the most of who we are. Moreover, whenever you try to imitate someone else, you are killing your creative self. You are your own **unique** person and as such, your life as evidenced by your actions should also be uniquely different from others.

You must learn to rely on yourself - your inner self

 In order to begin to secure a life of happiness, you must first dare to be an individual. You have to be able to say, "I would rather be disliked for who I am, than to be loved for who I am not". Not only must you be able to say it, you must also mean it. I think that if you take a look at those individuals in history who have made a difference in the world, you will see that, they were usually people who had to stand alone in the beginning. Their first act of courage was when they decided to stay on their course in spite of those around them who said it was not possible. They were committed to listening to the inner signals they were receiving. Usually these are the people who succeed.

To begin a life of happiness, you have to be comfortable being in your own skin, then and only then can you begin to live life.

Secondly, to secure a life of happiness, you must make a conscious choice – a definite choice of what you want out of life. Thirdly, you have to have a conscious knowledge of self.

Knowledge of self is a conscious awareness of who you are, and the power you possess.

Knowledge of self understands that: my body is a vessel for a spirit energy which lives inside of me, a part of my Creator called the gift of Life. Knowledge of self understands that I am essentially a spiritual being having a human experience and my journey will not end here on Earth. Knowledge of self understands that everything is created with thought. Mind power is the real key to success in life on all levels. When we come into a true knowledge of self, we understand that, through the power of our thinking, we are able to accomplish great things. When we come into a true knowledge of self, we begin to understand that the key to success rest with the individual and it all depends on the person.

This is what the Apostle Paul meant when he said in Ephesians 3-20 "And now unto Him who is able to

do exceeding abundantly above all that we ask or think according to the power that works in us" He was saying that the power lives inside of us.

This is one of <u>the Great Secrets of Life</u>. It would be a good idea to practice saying to yourself on a regular basis, "I <u>hold the key and it all depends on me</u>".

When we become consciously aware of the power that works in us, we begin to realize that we can pull ourselves out of any negative situation we are presently in. This is accomplished with the power of our mind, that's how it's done. That's how it has always been done. Any person, who has ever achieved success in life, has done so by the power of thinking and making up their mind to change their present condition. They made a decision, created a plan and were committed to seeing it through.

With the power of our mind, we can be what we want to be, get what we desire or accomplish whatever we are striving for. The only power to make success a reality in our life lives within us. When we become aware of its existence, we can consciously bring it forth and put it to work for us. It is with the power of the gift we possess inside that we are able to lift ourselves out of ANY RUT we are presently in.

However, in order to use the power you possess inside of you, you will have to grow up. No one can do your growing for you but you. You are the only one who can grow into the knowledge of who you are and the power you possess. You and only you can choose to use the power within you which can place you among the world's most respected and admired people. **It is the thinkers of**

**the world who are not victims of life but are creators
of their future.**

Confidence is the key to your success.

Your confidence must be the same confidence you used
when you had a strong desire for anything in your past that
you finally got. It may have been materialistic or romantic,
whatever it was, you got it by determination and confidence
in your abilities to make it a reality. This is no different.

If you will recall, you probably said in your mind and felt in
your heart, I'm going to get that and you did. You believed
and you did not doubt that you would have it one day and
that day did come. You were using the law of your being
and you were not consciously aware of it.

When you begin to understand the law of your being and
how the power inside you works,

you learn to be confident. Confidence gives you the ability
to practice patience, knowing that your success is on the
way. When you are able to do that, then nothing will be
impossible for you to achieve.

**We are responsible for our own actions "WE REAP
WHAT WE SOW"** Whatever actions we commit, whether
in thought or deeds, will return to us. . Throughout
history, in various countries around the world, the mystery
of this knowledge is made known. It is recognized in
most world religions, including Buddhism, Hinduism
and Christianity. Buddhists know it as the law of karma.
Hindis know it as the circle of fate or what goes around
comes around. And Christians know it as whatever you
sow you will reap. It is amazing that although these

religions profess different beliefs, they all agree on this universal spiritual law.

Accordingly, to illustrate how the law works, let's begin by taking a look at the farming process.

For argument sake, we will start with a farm and we will call the owner, farmer John.

Farmer John makes his living by growing crops. His process is quite simple. He cultivates the soil, and plants the desired seeds. After his seeds are planted, he starts the care of them by watering them on as regular basis. They are also nurtured by the rays of the sun. He examines the ground regularly to ensure that weeds are not taking root, which will choke the life out of his plants.

Each day he goes into the field with the expectation that the seeds are growing under the ground and that sooner or later they will become visible to the eye. After his crops sprout up, he trusts that they will continue to grow until such time as they are deemed ripe for the harvest.

Farmer John's process is exactly the same as our mental process; the only difference is that we are using our thought energy to bring change into our lives. We cultivate the soil of our soul with positive wholesome thoughts. These are thoughts which help, enhance and promote life. The healthier our thoughts are, the better demonstration we will have. It is through our thought process and the power of choice, that we begin to plant our desire. After planting a desire, we should begin to water our desires with a spirit of confidence, gratitude and thanksgiving.

Moreover, when we entertain positive thoughts, we allow spiritual energy to flow freely throughout our body, which has the same effect that rays of sun have on physical seeds.

You must learn to think positive, say to yourself and know in your heart, whatever you desire" it's on the way".

When we learn to expect our desires before they are actually seen, we are now learning to use powerful spiritual laws. In this instance it is called the law of expectancy.

<u>When we understand the law of expectancy, we give thanks because we come to fully expect that our continued thoughts along with work ,on what we desire, will become a reality.</u>

Moreover, it will not be enough to just think about changing your present condition or achieving success, you have to take action in the direction of your desires and dreams. **<u>"Faith without works according to the Bible is dead"</u>. <u>James 2-17</u>**

Also, if you will notice, once Farmer John plants his seeds, he does not dig them up the next day to see if they are taking root. Those kinds of actions would kill his efforts. Therefore, neither should we dig up our desires with doubt and fear. **<u>Doubt, fear, and thoughts of "what if this happens or what if that doesn't happen", only serve to create weeds of destruction. They weaken our focus and there by lessen our commitment to see our desires and dreams come true.</u>**

LEARN TO BE PATIENT.

It is important to remember that there is **always a space of time** between planting seeds, growing and the actual harvest of your crops, so you must learn to be patient. Your spiritual process is no different. Once your desires are planted by your thoughts, it will take time before you see actual results. Patience is a key ingredient and when we are patient, we learn to wait without worrying. We have inner assurance that everything will work out for the better.

I have found that this knowledge has the power to help you change your life. It will make your goals and dreams a reality, but it has to be lived. In order to live it, you have to abandon your old ideas and make room for new ones. **It is by renewing our minds with changed positive thinking that we become new creatures.**

Consider this:

If you always do what you have always done, you will get nothing but what you always got."

If you want something different in your life it stands to reason that, you will have to do something different.

If you give this information a chance, you will see that you have nothing to lose except the negative thinking and behaviors which are preventing you from achieving happiness and prosperity.

Steps to securing a life of happiness:

1. Learn to accept and appreciate who you are.

2. Learn to think positive.

3. Decide what you want out of life.

4. Understand the nature of your spirit.

5. Learn to be responsible for you.

6. Learn to expect to receive the things you desire.

7. Learn to be patient.

CHAPTER # 2

"Man's mind stretched to a new idea never goes back to its original dimensions"
Oliver Wendell Holmes

Who am I?

Three simple words, who am I. If I asked that simple question to the majority of people, most would start by saying, "I am a man or I am a woman" and of course they would undoubtedly include their ethnic background, black, white, Hispanic, oriental etc. etc. etc. They would be measuring and judging who they are by what their eyes could see. However, most people don't have a clue about who they really are.

Now if you are asking; "if I am more than the physical body I see when I look in the mirror, what part of me am I not seeing"? That would be a good question because I believe if you can understand this then you are well on your way to changing your life for the better. Accordingly, man is more than the physical body. Man has a triune nature. He has three parts in one. Man is made up of a mind, body and spirit all in one. It is the physical body that houses the mind and spirit.

I think at this point, we can agree on these facts:

(A) We possess a body and (B) we all possess a mind, otherwise we could not think. However, when it comes to understanding the spirit of man, this required that I do a little investigation.

Accordingly, when I researched the idea of the spirit part of man; I found extensive works in Christian, Islamic and Judaic religions. These religions teach that man has a living spirit inside of him. Many people refer to it as "the life force" or "the invisible spiritual energy" which allows us to live. These religions teach that the spirit of man is actually a part of our Creator, and because He loved man so much, His greatest act of showing that love, was to place a part of Himself in each and every human being.

And just as a man's body could not function well without proper food and water, it is also a fact that man would be incomplete without properly caring for his mind, body, and spirit.

Therefore, in order to enjoy a healthy and prosperous life, mind, body and spirit must be nurtured and maintained, thus creating a well balanced man.

Promoting a healthy Mind

In order to promote a healthy mind, it is essential that we feed it. The mind is one of the key components needed in making our realities what we want them to be.

We achieve our goals by using the power of our minds. Therefore, in order to effectively use our mind, we have to nurture it by continuously feeding it knowledge. And since knowledge is infinite, the supply is inexhaustible. We have to be able to take time out of our busy day to read a book or watch a television program which is informative. We should try to learn something new each day that can be used in life. Learn to exercise your mind by quietly observing your surrounding or any situation which will increase your analytical ability. Growth is a natural process in the life of man. The more knowledge (know-how) that the mind receives, the more it will grow. In light of this, we should always experience those things which promote a healthy mind and in doing so, we increase our potential for great accomplishments. It is through positive life experiences that we are motivated to experience more.

Components of a healthy body:

Now as it relates to the physical body, the body is nourished by a supply of proper:

(1) FOOD

(2) EXERCISE

(3) SLEEP

I would like to take a few minutes to discuss the importance of each separately.

Food

We live in a fast tracked society which thrives on fast food. Many people in the hurriedness of their lives fall victim to fast foods and snacks. The problem with this is that although these foods taste good, they usually contain little or no nutritional value. Our body's make up is complex and that being the case; we need balanced nutrients to maintain a healthy body. When we choose to buy fast foods on the run, we give up the benefit our bodies would receive from more natural foods.

It is a proven fact that most snacks and many fast foods contain chemicals, additives and preservatives which are no good for human consumption-notice I said no good, not toxic. These foods have little or no nutritional value. The body needs food with balanced nutrients to be healthy and beautiful. Proper nutrients help the body fight disease. They also help the body in its maintenance and healing process. It is no wonder that, we live in a nation where a large majority of the population is plagued with illnesses, which are clearly preventable. Much of their poor health is due to the food choices they make. These bad food choices are the leading causes of obesity, high blood pressure and heart disease. The list goes on and on. Generally my personal choice is, if it has no nutritional value, I avoid it.

I remember before I decided to change my life, I used to eat in and everything. Whatever they were selling in the store, if I became enticed by it, I usually purchased it and needless to say, I also ate it.

As a result of eating all of those crazy foods, I would usually wake-up the next morning feeling bloated with gas. Let me not forget mentioning, my weight was also out of control. Now that I have become consciously aware of the idea of eating foods which are low in calories and fat, I now wake up feeling refreshed. As a result of better food choices, I lost weight and I no longer get that bloated uncomfortable feeling in the morning. If we decide to make the choice to live healthier life styles by avoiding foods which are high in calories, fats and sugars, most of us would escape the illnesses that are associated with a poor diet. This all goes back to our thinking and the choices we make for our lives. We must learn to think in terms of promoting life and these foods certainly do not promote life. On the contrary, they are associated with shortening our life expectancy.

Exercise

Exercise is by far the single most important decision we can make to promote good health and fight off disease. It is my sincere contention as supported by our medical community that a regular exercise routine will help to promote good physical and mental health. It will also fight obesity. A regular exercise routine also reduces our chances of getting high blood pressure, diabetes, cancer, and heart disease.

I remember on one occasion consulting my mother about an exercise program I was considering, and her response to me was "son you have to take care of your body, because you will not be getting another one".

I thought that was sound advice, so I am passing it on to you. **"You have to take care of your body because, you will not be getting another one".**

Also have you ever noticed how a person who exercises on a regular basis look, I have? These people usually have a vibrant, youthful appearance and their energy levels are high.

SLEEP.

Another essential element to a healthy body is proper sleep. It is a fact that the body needs sufficient sleep each night if it is to be healthy, usually between 6 and 8 hours. On a number of occasions, I've had the opportunity to visit the correctional facilities in my area as a motivational speaker. Often I see inmates whose appearances are vibrant and radiant. Now these are individuals who are there for a number of offenses including drug abuse. They usually come into the prison really beat up. And after about four months of incarceration, their skin has cleared up, their hair looks healthy and they are glowing. One of the things I tell them is that when they look into the mirror, they are seeing what nature intended for them to look like.

I explain that because the toxins are gone, the body can start doing repair work. Now, when they sleep their body goes through a sleep process which is known as qualitative sleep. Before their incarceration, they were getting what is called quantitative sleep, meaning, although they were getting sleep, the body would use that time to clean up the toxins they were ingesting. It is no wonder that often they would wake up tired after sleeping for hours, simply because the body did not rest. It was doing a toxic clean-up job. Now, with the absence of toxins, the body does qualitative sleep. It can now work on beautifying itself. In short, they glow.

Now when I consider the question of who am I, in order to get a full appreciation of who am I, mind, body, and spirit must be nurtured. Moreover, if you are planning to experience a prosperous, abundant, healthy life, mind, body and spirit must be balanced.

<u>SPIRIT</u>

As we consider mind, body and spirit, the one we need to pay close attention to is the spirit. It is our spirit that carries the real power. However, for most people- the spirit has not been nurtured. It has been neglected and as with anything, if we do not nourish it, it becomes weak. This is one of the main reasons why people never realize their full potential. They neglect the triune nature and especially their spirit.

Spirit plays a major role in helping man to achieve his goals, dreams and acquire the material things he may desire. And what is it that makes the spirit so special and powerful? Well, if you will recall, earlier, I said that our spirit is a part of our Creator, which was given to us as a personal gift of love.

It is special and powerful because it is actually God inside of you. It is that teaspoon from the ocean. It is love. And since it is love, it serves to reason that in order to promote a healthy spirit; we must nourish it with love and positive life experiences. Many times in today's world, the word love is associated with some act of intimacy. Love does not always mean an intimate relationship with someone. The bounds of love are endless and are not restricted to only acts of intimate relations. One way we can bring love to our spirit would be by participating in an activity such as sports, dancing, enjoying your family or the love of education. Whenever you engage in an activity that is positive, you are feeding your spirit love.

Many times I've heard people say: I feel sad or empty and for no reason at all. Usually, their feelings border depression. And for the life of them, they cannot figure it out. Their conversation usually goes something like this: Something feels wrong but I just can't put my finger on it. After all, there is no real problem going on right now that would cause me to feel this way.

They do not understand that when they are experiencing these feelings, they are absolutely correct in saying that, something feels wrong.

What they are experiencing is a cry from their inner spirit asking to be fed.

The answer to their discomfort is simple. Their spirit needs to be fed and this can be done by doing something positive.

We are all part of this great universe. And scientists have long discovered that the universe is growing. They see that it is growing and they claim that they don't know why. Well, if they would study the spiritual aspects of things, they would soon discover that our great Creator makes things out of Himself. Spirit is always seeking expression. For the universe, spirit shows growth with the appearance of new planets and scientific phenomenon. However, human growth is demonstrated by the positive experiences we bring to life. Therefore, in our efforts to help our spirit grow, it is always a good idea to consciously seek out knowledge, which is inspirational. It has been my experience that whenever I read inspirational books, my energy level rises. Also, when we help others, we are feeding our spirit. In light of that, you could do something nice for someone who needs it, not expecting anything in return. When we help others by bringing joy and happiness into their lives, their joy and happiness returns to our own lives. The joy they send out as a result of our help to them, acts as rays of spiritual sunshine, thereby feeding our own spirits.

It is essential that we have a healthy spirit. We cannot neglect spirit if we are to be truly successful in all we set-out to accomplish. Moreover, we have to allow it to grow with continuous knowledge of truth and take that same truth and translate it into helping others. We should constantly seek to help out where ever we can. As we help others, we also help ourselves. It is in helping others that our spirit experiences the unconditional love it needs to grow and as our spirit grows within, we grow on the outside in grace and beauty.

Accordingly, you are probably aware of the fact that life always grows or decays from the inside out. It has been my experience that the outer appearance of a person more often than not will reflect their inner condition. If a person consistently express an outer appearance of well being, then it is certain that there is wellness in the inner life – their mind and spirit.

However, when I encounter individuals whose lives are full of confusion, these are usually clear indications of an inner life- mind and spirit, which are off balance and not in tune with the universe.

Jesus says in Matthews7:16"You will know them by their fruits". It is in our study of these truths that we begin to gain wisdom in our lives. As a result, if there is one thing I do know about people whose lives are full of confusion and drama, is that such individuals in their present state, are not about to accomplish anything positive.

A bad tree cannot produce good fruit until it has been pruned. And likewise, people experiencing a life of confusion and disharmony cannot create any positive, harmonious conditions, in their lives, until there is a change in their thinking. "We are transformed by the renewing of our minds" Romans 12:2

Another equally important point I would like to address with the question – "who am I", is Individuality. It saddens me to say that over the past years of my life, I've observed the behavior of people, especially our youth. As a result of this observation, it has become increasingly clear that most people lack the courage to be themselves. I have found that they are afraid of the present. They are afraid of the future. They are afraid of death and they are afraid of each other. They are afraid to express who they are and what they really feel. For the most part, people have become accustomed to listening to what other people around them are saying

and doing. As a result, without any fore thought of their own, they simply jump on the band wagon.

Whether it's true or not, they are off and running. __They become a part of the "ME TOO" club.__ What people fail to realize is, whenever you act in a way that takes your individuality, you are hindering and killing your spirit. That divine part of you that makes you who you are. Each person on the planet is a unique expression of our Creator. This great universe we live in is doing many great and wonderful things right now. You are one of the things the universe is doing right now. No one can express your greatness, uniqueness or your individuality but you. Therefore, when you try to be someone you are not, you give- up the right to be yourself.

Moreover, let's say people do accept you-while you are wearing your mask. You are depriving them of getting to know the real you. You are apparently afraid to be yourself and for what. Are you feeling that you have something to hide? Whatever it is, you either have to let it out by being yourself, or find friends who will accept you for who you really are. In denying your true self, you are stunting your personal and spiritual growth.

When you are not being yourself, you are living a lie. And who wants to live a lie simply because they are afraid to be who they are? We all have a divine right to be who we are without exception.

There are far too many people in the world today, who are living below their possibilities because they have given up their right to be an individual. __If you want to live a life with power, then be yourself__. You have a right to be who you are. **No one has the right to define who you are but __you.__**

As it relates to the strength involved in being yourself, your strength will come from your ability to allow others the right to be who they are as well. **Acceptance is the key; remember "it is what it is".**

You must have acceptance in your life. Each person is an individual, and that being so, it is spiritually wholesome when we allow all viewpoints, without feeling the need to defend our point of view. Our way of looking at the situation is not the only way.

None the less, you cannot allow anyone to tell you what your journey must reflect or what your reality is. Do not give the power to be yourself away so easily, but give your love unconditionally. Also, remember that low self esteem is just as non -productive as a puffed up sense of self esteem, they are two sides of the same coin. We have to rid ourselves of the more than and less than complexes. They are equally destructive.

For me, I have decided to take this position: It is not important if I am liked by people or not. Of course, it would be nice to be accepted and treated nice. Unfortunately, most people do not know what they like. They change their likes and dislikes like the wind blows.

The most important thing for me, is not whether people like or dislike me, but more importantly, do I like me. If I do not like myself, how can I expect anyone else to like me? Therefore, learning to love and like oneself, is the first order of business.

CHAPTER #3

"Whatever your life's work is, do it well. A man should do his job so well that the living, the dead and the unborn could do it no better"

Martin Luther King Jr.

A Life Of Purpose

I believe that most people without exception want to be happy. They just can't figure out what they should be doing to make happiness a reality. For me, the single most important decision I made which helped me experience a happier, more joyful life, was the day I decided to search for my purpose in life. I believe it is not by accident that we are here at this time and place. It is also my contention that we are here on purpose and with a purpose. Everyone has a purpose in life, even if they are not aware of it. **<u>Our purpose in life, is to live a life of purpose</u>**. During our conception, the Creator endowed us with the power of Himself. His intent was that we should bring this energy into the world to serve others. **We were all given unique gifts and special talents, which we must share with others.** When we are able to identify our talents and gifts and use them to help others, we are living a life of purpose. This is our reason for being here.

However, it seems to me that most people travel on the sea of life without ever attempting to know their purpose in life.

They seldom ask these simple questions:

1. WHY AM I HERE?

2. WHAT IS MY PURPOSE IN LIFE?

Without ever exploring any other possibilities for themselves, people simply drift. They do not possess enough inner strength to follow their own creative self. They do not understand and appreciate their own uniqueness.

Instead, they become victim to what everyone else is doing. Moreover, they usually continue to be caught up in this aimless drifting, until one day, they look around and notice that years have passed. They also notice that from one year to the next, they have remained the same. There has been no advancement made in their lives, in any direction.

History bears witness of people present and past, who just could not get their lives together. They were never able to get in tune with the universe. They never understood that we were sent here to shine like the many stars we see in the heavens. And the way that we shine, is when we use the talents and gifts we were given to help others.

A Life of Purpose Has Nothing to Do with Money.

Although money is a security, there is a lot of truth to the old saying "money is not everything".

The acquisition of prosperity and living life with a purpose, are altogether two different things.

It is my experience that a life of purpose is a life where a conscious choice is made to pursue a constructive endeavor.

It involves having a reason to get out of bed every day to pursue your goals. To live life with a purpose means that you have decided what you want out of life or what you want to achieve. Moreover, you have made a commitment to see your goals and dreams become a reality.

When I consider a life of purpose, I am reminded of a time in my life where I believed that my purpose in life was to: use drugs day in and day out. And when I was not using drugs, I was thinking of ways to get more. Drugs would be the first thing I did in the morning and the last thing I did at night. Every day after I got my drugs, I would feel empty, as though something was missing.

 I could not be content no matter how much I used. Day by day the void inside of me deepened.

Every morning, I would see busses full of people on their way to work. I often found myself wondering what it would feel like to have a job again. I usually spent my day casting about.

Many times, I would think about the condition of my life and begin to cry. The fact that I was throwing my life away, trapped off by drugs, nearly destroyed me physically, and emotionally.

Countless nights, rain, sleet or snow, it did not matter, I would be out there on the streets well pass 12 or 1 o'clock, looking for ways to get drugs. Often, I waited for the local bars to close.

I waited, because I knew the people leaving the bars would be drunk. I played on their sympathy and drunkenness to get the money I needed. Many nights I found myself alone on dark streets.

It was during those times, when I was alone on dark streets late at night, that I was forced to look at myself. I was forced to see the naked truth. The truth was that I was lost and needed help. The truth was that deep inside, I knew I could never feel good about myself as long as I continued to use drugs. The truth was that drugs and my selfish way of life had separated me from the one thing I loved most on the entire planet, my family. Many times, I longed for a guardian angel or some great power to deliver me from my despair.

It was on those nights, when I would have moments of clarity, that I would pray and ask God to save me from myself. My exact words were "save me Lord, from myself. I am counting on You, because I cannot do it alone, I need your help". It was on those cold, lonely, desperate nights that my only desire was "Lord Please turn this entire horrific nightmare around to your glory one day". Although I could not see how it could ever happen, I wanted my useless existence to one day become a positive message that would help others. I believed that if I could be granted that blessing, then all of my suffering would not have been in vain. One of my greatest fears was the possibility that I would die without accomplishing my purpose in life, my reason for coming to earth in the first place. I did not want to die in my addiction. And from all indication on those nights, I believed that I was too far gone to change and the final solution for me would have to be death. As far as I could see, there was no other way out.

It is a great tragedy when a person is so caught up in the madness of life, that they truly believe in their heart that there is no hope, and death is their only solution. One thing I noticed was that people generally showed less compassion in matters which they have never experienced. If anyone could have experienced the madness of my life in those days, they would know the meaning of "having compassion for others". They would understand that compassion, simply put, is having the ability to imagine yourself in the other person's condition of pain and suffering.

It was by the grace of God and through His divine guidance, that I finally made it to a drug recovery program. It was there that I first entertained the thought of: if I am not going to use drugs any more, then what will I do, day in and day out. I knew that I had to replace the drug time with doing something positive now that I was clean. In my search for a purpose in life, I began to talk to people who were in recovery. I asked them how they occupied their time now that the drugs were gone.

They all had different suggestions, but one thing they did suggest was that I consider doing something to make amends for my past community actions. In my personal story, if you will remember, I said that there was a time in my life when drugs had reduced me to a lying scam artist. What I did not mention was the fact that the victims of my scams were usually unsuspecting parents who believed that I worked for an organization that was committed to help in the fight against drug abuse, and gang violence.

Now that my obsession to use drugs had been removed, on the advice of fellow recovering addicts, I decided to return to my home town. Now that I was clean, I wanted to make a sincere effort to somehow make amends for my past actions. I wanted to show God, the community and myself that, although, I had wronged people to get money for my drugs, the truth was that I really did have a strong desire to help. That was probably one of the reasons I was so successful in my scam. It was because people could see something in me that spoke beyond my present condition. They saw a measure of truth in my words.

 The only problem was that as a result of my addiction, I was not able to make it a reality. Now that I was on the road to recovery, there existed the real possibility, that I might one day live a life of purpose, by helping others_

How to pursue a life of purpose

The first thing you will need to live a life of purpose is a desire to do something. I think we can agree that to accomplish anything worthwhile, you must have a strong desire. It has to be something that you really want to do. Our inner spirit seeks to create, it is our nature. And since creation begins with our thoughts, fueled by spiritual power, to live life with purpose is our individual self -expression inspired by spirit. People have to realize that our purpose for coming to the planet is to help others. It is true that we were sent here to enjoy the life experience, but we were also sent here to work, by helping others. As it relates to helping others, I believe when we are willing to assist others, the power of the spirit helps us in accomplishing our goals. I remember on one occasion in my life, I worked in a grammar school as a substitute teacher, in the city of Paterson N.J. On this particular day, I visited a fellow teacher, and noticed that the teacher was conducting a reading group. I also noticed that there was one student sitting in the corner of the room. When I looked at him, I noticed, he appeared to be angry. I asked the teacher "what's his problem"? She informed me that he was disruptive and unwilling to participate in the group. Immediately, I looked at him with disappointment.

At which time, in a stern voice, I asked him to get up and come to me. He did not move. Instead he stayed in his seat and gave no indication that he was going to respond to my demand. Somehow, I knew something was wrong. As result, I decided to ask him again, except this time, I extended both my arms and opened my hands in a loving and caring manner. My action prompted him to respond different this time. He must have sensed the sincerity in me. This time he got up out of his seat, came to me and placed his hands in mine. When he did, I asked him "What's wrong little brother"? He told me that the other children did not want him around them. He said that he slept in the bed with his younger brother, who wet the bed and the scent was on him. He further stated that the other children were making fun of him. He said they were calling him "pissy". When he told me that, I asked the teacher would it be ok for him to come out of the classroom with me. She responded "Yes! You can take him any where you want, just take him out of here". I felt his pain and as a result, I was eager to help out. I remembered that there were donated clothes in the nurses' office, so that was our first stop. When we reached her office, there was a box of donated clothes. I began looking for clothes to fit him and amazingly, the very first pair of pants and shirt we found were a perfect fit. I had him go into the bathroom and wash his body off, while I guarded the door. When he emerged from the bathroom, he had a new smile of confidence on his face. I asked him, "Are you ready to return to your class to learn something"? He responded with a hearty "yes"!!!

When we reached the classroom, he immediately opened his book with eager anticipation. I informed the teacher that she would not have any more trouble with him. And as I was about to leave the classroom, I heard someone call me," Mr. Matthews" and when I looked back to see who it was, it was the student, only this time he smiled and winked. I felt, he appreciated my efforts. He warmed my heart. His gesture indicated that we had come to an understanding. He no longer felt like an outcast, he was now a part of the class. I shared that story with you to illustrate the power of spirit when we are willing to help others. How is it that, when we reached the nurse's office, the very clothes we sought, were there waiting for us? We didn't even have to search for them. I believe, when we make an effort to help others, spirit will orchestrate the situation in a way where the outcome will always be in our favor.

It is also important to understand that, when we are helping others, our own spirit grows from the experience. There is a desire in our spirit. It wants to be expressed and it is more readily expressed when we are helping others. Consequent to that, we all have come to the planet with a specific intent. There is an intended purpose for everything on the planet and, we are no different.

As we come into the knowledge of truth about our true identity: we begin working to create conditions that promote and enhance life starting with ourselves, and then others.

It is equally important to know that in order to live an effective life of purpose; you will need wisdom and understanding to guide you. Wisdom and understanding are spiritual in nature. And, since we are spiritual beings, we cannot expect to accomplish anything worthwhile without wisdom and understanding. In the hands of wisdom and understanding lie riches, long life, peace and happiness**. In our search for purpose, we come to understand that we will receive through faith all the wisdom and understanding we**

need when we ask from our heart three simple words: Father Help Me.

I recently heard a story in which I was so intrigued that; I feel I must share with you. According to the story, we all made an agreement with God to come to Earth to take on the challenges placed in our lives. As a result, many of the challenges we encounter are designed to help us in our spiritual growth and journey. It is as though in the agreement, God said He would give us a free will and whatever choices we made, He would respect. It was also agreed that: **God would not interfere in our lives, unless we asked for His help**. Often times, our greatest source of strength comes in the form of our ability to humble ourselves and ask for help. It is through wisdom and understanding that we come to the realization that we do need help.

Many people lack wisdom and understanding, and it is for this reason in the bible, the book of James 4:2 It says "You have not, because you ask not" and it also says in James 1:5 "if any of you lack wisdom let him ask God. Therefore; for anyone who believes they lack wisdom and understanding, they should ask God for wisdom and understanding to guide them in life.

As you look up into the sky, you will notice that, we are not inside the Earth; on the contrary, we are on the surface. It therefore stands to reason that we are an active part of this great universe and as such, when we align ourselves with It, any supply we need to help us in our purpose through faith, we will receive. To quote Joseph Campbell, "it is as though a thousand hands will drop from heaven to assist you when you are trying to do what's right". However, our first purpose in life has to be, to take responsibility for our own lives and the lives that we helped to bring into the world.

Although, to live a life of purpose is the most rewarding life a person could pursue, many times, as was the case with me, people feel trapped by their present conditions.

Often people are living in conditions and under circumstances which they would like to see changed. What they must understand is that, the only way they can change the effect, is by first changing the cause. **It is the law of Cause and Effect. Consequently, it is their thinking that has to change, if they are going to change any outer condition.**

Thinking is the key to change.

People live in situations of poverty and lack, because every minute of the day, they concentrate and focus on what they do not have.

As a result of this kind of thinking, they continue in their hardship, sickness and poverty. They say that they want a better life, but their thoughts are so focused on the negativity of what they do not have, the result is that, they'll never have a chance for anything better.

By their own thinking, they are defeated and this is because they do not understand their creative nature. You must change your thinking. You should start thinking about the things that you do want, say in your spirit and believe in your heart: one day I will have it. You have to learn to expect the best out of life. Look for the best in people. You cannot receive good, while expecting evil. You cannot expect prosperity while looking for poverty and you cannot expect success when you are walking around looking like a failure.

We share a part of the divine nature, we are creators by birth; it is therefore the Power of the Gift inside of you, which can make or break you. You are what you think and there is no getting around that.

We create our own conditions.

In order to engage in a life of purpose, you have got to do something. You have got to find a way to pull yourself out of that rut you are in. You have to stop existing and start living. What must be done is this: you have got to identify and use the talents that GOD has given you **to help yourself and others.** We were sent here as builders, to help change the world by making it a better place. To change the world does not mean that you have to be some world known person with this great following. To change the world is as simple as this: If you helped to bring truth to one person- you just changed the world for the better.

Moreover, do you recall the story in the bible about the talents? It states that the one man who went off and hid his talent was not favored, but those who made use of their talents were given an increase. They were put in charge of greater things. When you look at that story, you see how it is that, as you use the talents that were given to you by God, like anything else, you get better at it. Practice makes perfect. It only serves to reason that there will be an increase in your skill and ability, thereby making success an even greater possibility.

You too, have the opportunity to increase your talents by using them. By using your talents and gifts you will open even greater doors in your life, but in order to do that, you have to use them.

What you must realize is that no matter what you feel your personal gifts or talents are; only action brings them to life. <u>It is by doing that you will come to understand what is possible.</u>

For that reason, to live a life of purpose, would be to use the talents which have been placed in your hands to help yourself and others. Jesus said "thou shall love the Lord Thy God". This is the first and greatest commandment. It is when we use the talents that God has placed in our hands in the most positive way; that we show our love for Him. <u>**Whatever we set out to do, whatever goal we pursue, we can accomplish. Whatever purpose in life we set-out to achieve is attainable through the power of the gift, which is activated through our thinking. If you really understand that you can achieve all that you desire, then success for you is just a matter of time**</u>. You are now coming into the knowledge of the truth.

In our pursuit for a life of purpose, we learn to appreciate the fact that we are all connected directly to the only power in the entire Universe, who possess all Knowledge (know-How) all Wisdom and Understanding. Moreover, He is willing to share everything with you. Whatever you may need to accomplish your purpose in life, will be given to you.

All you have to do is really need something for the good of life and believe that you have it, and you will have it. The most high God is a no limit God, and as a result, the only limit that can be placed on you, will come from you. **Any limit you place on yourself will be due to your lack of faith and vision.**

How do you find your purpose in life ?

Although everyone has a different purpose in life, finding your purpose in life, is an individual endeavor. However, there are a few suggestions which may lead you to your purpose in life. It is suggested that you start by listening to your inner voice. It is the power of the gift inside of you which will guide you into your purpose in life. Usually our first indication of our purpose in life is to take notice of those things that make you feel good when you are doing them. Recently, I had a conversation with a young man who shared with me his experience of speaking with a sixth grade class about gang violence and drug abuse. He commented that after his talk with them he felt very good about himself. I said to him "that would be the kind of indication one would look for when trying to determine what ones purpose in life is". **Also, notice what your talents are.** Many times, I have encountered people who say to me that they are not sure what their talents are. My response to them is usually, "well, what do you enjoy doing"? I have found that talent is usually what you like to do, if you like doing a particular activity; chances are you are going to be talented at it. **Once you have found your talents, you have to use them to help others.** Even the measure of a king is how well he serves his subjects. Doctors, Lawyers, Teachers, even our Garbage Collectors all serve. They give of their time and services. They are active participants in life, and they work in a way that helps others in the advancement of life. You must serve humanity that is the secret and key to living a life of purpose.

You can create a life of purpose.

Look around you right now. How can you serve those around you? Any man, who has a full appreciation for the law of his being and the law of attraction, understands that he can only get back what he gives but multiplied, and with this knowledge, he can begin to create for himself a life of purpose. Accordingly, the more you think about the law of attraction, the more you will understand exactly how it works. When we come into the knowledge of our true selves, we began to engage in a purpose which helps by offering our service to others. The Law of Attraction works to serve us. When we learn to use it intelligently, we place ourselves in a position where all that we desire is possible. Everything we think generates a force of energy that returns to us in like kind.

That is what is meant in the words "**we reap what we sow**" and to the point that we serve others, will this same law serve us in supplying us with whatever we need to live and prosper.

Another great thing about living a life-of purpose is that, it produces physical and spiritual growth. As we grow spiritually and physically, we begin to get a greater appreciation for life.

Start a life of purpose by letting your light shine.

One way to begin a life of purpose is to always present yourself in a way that you are an inspiration to others. Whenever you are exposed to the general public, you are sending some kind of signal, you cannot help it. To everybody who looks at you, you are communicating a message. **They look at you before you even open your mouth, first impressions are lasting**. . We should therefore learn to be inspirational. Learn to advertise life which is vibrant, energetic and blissful.

In our search for a life of purpose, it is our reasonable service to project an image which serves to build up, and encourage those around us. We should aspire to be an asset, not a liability to our brothers and sisters.

Furthermore, there is nothing like a genuine smile. **A smile is to humans as, oil is to machinery, it loosens them up**, therefore, if we offer genuine smiles, we are sure to receive the same in kind, only multiplied. Even if the smile is not returned, we should be ok with that, because, we did what we wanted to do. We did not do it expecting to receive anything in return. Besides, we can smile in confidence because we know who we are. We are children of the King, sons and daughters of the Most High God. So why should we not smile?

In a life of purpose, the real key is service and giving. Is it not written in Acts 20:35 that "it is better to give than to receive"? It stands to reason, that only if we are willing to give of ourselves, will we find a prosperous, happy and successful life. It is when we pursue a life of purpose that we are acting in accord with the law of our being.

This law works whether we are aware of it or not, whether we believe it or not. When we are serving others, we are operating in the law of love. When we operate within the law of love, we place ourselves in a win win situation. You cannot break the law of love, and expect to live a life of happiness and prosperity. Ignorance of the law is no excuse. **You must comply with the law of your being.**

Therefore, in your conclusion, you may say "I believe what you are saying, but what do I have to offer? What can I give?" You can start with a gift of your knowledge, your time, or any idea you may have, which would make life better for someone else. That would be a great place to start. Even more simple, start by giving smiles to those you meet in your travels.

Remember, the key to a successful life of purpose, is a life where we are serving others. When we serve we give and when we give, we are using a law that will not fail, it cannot fail because, it is law.

How to pursue your purpose in life?

1. You need to have a strong desire to accomplish something.

2. Pray for wisdom and understanding.

3. Identify and use your gifts and talents.

4. Determine what you can do to help others.

5. Understand and apply the law of attraction to your life..

6. Learn to let your light shine.

CHAPTER # 4

"Every time a value is born, existence takes on a new meaning; every time a value dies, some part of that meaning passes away"

Joseph Wood Krutch

<u>Where do I start?</u>

A few years ago, the singer Michael Jackson sang a song that said **"if you want to make the world a better place, take a look at yourself, and make a change".** He said, we should start with the "man in the mirror". Essentially he was right, because all lasting change must come from the individual himself.

<u>You will have to start with yourself.</u>

I have found that people are anxious to change their lives, but are unwilling to change and improve themselves. In order to change your life, you must start by honestly answering the following questions.

1. Does it make sense to change from my present condition?

2. Do I believe this is something that I can do?

3. What benefits would I receive if I do change?

4. How will the change make my life different?

These four questions must be asked and answered with complete honesty. Honesty is important, because it is a fact that people will not change anything in their lives, unless it makes sense to change. And when they honestly believe that change is necessary, it is then that they apply their entire being to making the change a reality. You cannot expect to achieve success in anything if you do not honestly believe you can do it. You must believe in your cause. Once you come to the conclusion that you can be successful, it's just a matter of starting.

When I look back at my stay in Bath, N.Y., as it relates to deciding to change, I am reminded of a situation where my honest determination to change prevailed. The situation was that, I had been in the program for about three months. During that time, I made it a habit to call my parents every week. On this particular occasion, I had just finished my work-out at the gym, and decided to give them a call. My mother answered the phone and immediately, I could tell something was bothering her. Once I made my usual greeting, she asked me a question which went something like "has anyone bothered you up there"? Of course, she got my attention and my response to her was "no why". At that point, she gave the phone to my father, who was apparently given the job of making things clear to me. As soon as he got on the phone his first remark was "the sheriff department was here looking for you". Now that was clear, crystal clear. "The sheriff department, I repeated" I knew if the sheriff department came looking for me, that was Superior Court and it had to be serious. My next question to him was "did you tell them where I am"? And although I was not surprised, his response was "yes, I told them". Needless to say, at that point, my day had taken a turn for the worst. My father said that the officer had left a contact number, and that I should give him a call. I wrote down the number and gave the officer a call. I called right away and when I reached him, he informed me that the warrant was due to me not paying a fine, and if I could get a certain amount of money to them, they could have the warrant lifted, otherwise, they would do what had to be done. After speaking to the officer, I immediately called my parents back and told them the outcome. I asked them if they had money to lend me to meet my present need. Their response was that they did not have any money to help me. At that point, all I could do was to relax and breathe. I was not sure if the sheriff department would be coming for me or not. But what I was sure of was that I was serious about changing my life. At that point, I determined in my spirit that, I would not worry. If they did decide to come for me, I would willingly go with them and as soon as the matter was settled, I would return to the program to complete what I set out to do, "recover from my drug addiction" and change my life.

After accepting that fact in my spirit, I simply reclined in the chair I was sitting in and began to listen to my music. To my surprise, the next thing I knew, one of my fellow veteran brothers tapped me on my shoulders and asked me to have a cup of coffee with him. As soon as I saw who it was, I started planning my pitch.

I remembered that he had mentioned to me a week earlier that he had received $96,000.00 from the V.A., disability dept. Boy was I relieved. I knew he would lend me the money and he did.

My point in sharing that story with you was that, although things were looking bleak for a moment, once I made the decision to change my life, I was committed to seeing it through. **I was not about to give up on my decision to**

change. I believed in my decision enough to actually go to jail, and upon my release, return to the recovery facility to continue the process of changing my life. I also believe that because I was serious about my recovery, God had sent me help. How is it that that person came at that time, when I needed his assistance most? Why him, why not someone else. Spirit is aware of all things. It will be no different for you, when you decide to change your life for the better. I believe, when we set out to do the right thing in life, spirit will help us in our cause.

Getting Started

We start by making a choice; remember, people succeed at whatever they set their mind to.   Whatever you decide to do, you must do it for yourself first, only then can you help others. **Do it with a sincere heart and a well made up mind.** Now that you have decided to do something, you should imagine yourself fulfilling your dream. Use your imagination. Our imagination is one of the greatest gifts we have. It is spiritual in nature, and is used to set a mold in place from which the law of attraction can work. It is through our spiritual nature that we move toward but not beyond what we think and imagine. From your imagination, you are telling the law of attraction what you want things to be like. Imagine it in your heart and mind.   Try to imagine what it would feel like when you have succeeded. Try to make your whole body, mind, and spirit feel the joy of your success.

And why is this so important?   Well, remember, we are made in the image of our Creator, and there is a part of Him in each of us. That part of Him inside of us has not and will not lose its creative nature. Therefore, when we use our imagination, and attach feelings to our desires, we set vibrations in motion which are acted upon by the law of attraction. The law of attraction mirrors back to us exactly what we send out, only multiplied. So when you send out images of a changed condition accompanied by feelings, you are sending a message which says to the law of attraction, this is what I want, send more, and make this my reality. The law of attraction does not analyze and say I'll send you more of this but not that, nor does it judge. The law of attraction is a precise law. **People do not attract into their lives what they just say they want; they attract what they desire and feel on the inside**. All creation starts on the inside of the individual. **<u>"As a man thinketh in his heart, so is he"</u>**. Therefore, if you want to be successful, you should be thinking about success. The law of attraction only gives man what he sends out. The law of attraction is a law which is given to us to serve and to help us. **<u>We can prosper, providing we use this law in a positive intelligent way; proper use is a matter of personal survival</u>**.

Many people in their lack of knowledge have, through wrong thinking, created disastrous conditions in their lives. This is why it is important that we learn to not only change our thinking, but also control our thinking. We are creators. It is a process that starts in our minds as a thought and then an action, which brings about consequences either positive or negative.

There is no getting around this fact – It is the law of our being. Therefore the man, who comes into the knowledge of truth, knows that <u>right thinking is an act of self preservation</u>. Moreover, I sincerely believe, if people really understood the power of their thoughts, they would be extremely careful about what thoughts they entertained. **That is why in the bible; Paul says in Philippians 4: 8 "Whatever things are**

honest, just, lovely, of a good report…. Think on these things".

He instructed this because he knew the law of our being, and he understood the power of thoughts. **And as we begin to think right thoughts, which are positive and wholesome, we become "new creatures" by the renewing of our minds". As supported in Romans 12:2, once our minds are renewed, only God knows what we can achieve. With all of that, the first step still must come from you. You have to choose to live a better life. There are many doors of opportunity in life and you hold the key that will open them. Your key is simply making a choice to enter them. It is with a strong desire, confident expectation and the courage to take action that you will be successful in making your dreams a reality.**

So again, when you ask the question "where do I start"? I say "Right where you are, right now".

Many times, I meet people who say, "you know, **I really would like to make a change in my life, But"….**

And almost always, without failure, the word "But" is followed by some kind of personal excuse. These excuses range from, I'm too old or I'm not smart enough. Or, I'm too young for that, I don't have the will power or the patience to do that. I thought about it, but ……Blah blah blah blah blah.

One thing people have to realize is that change is unavoidable. Change is something that you cannot change. We are always changing; this is part of our human nature. Whether positive or negative, the outcome is up to you. I think the real question is, "Am I going to guide my life with the power of my mind, body and spirit in the direction I choose, or am I going to allow myself to be a victim of circumstances, as oppose to creating them". You cannot allow yourself to aimlessly drift down the stream of life, without planning a destination, most people usually crash. You must decide how you want your life to be, and what you want out of life.

The one and only thing you have to win is success, and this is done with your mind. Respect it- Appreciate it, and most of all, Use it.

Remember that before you can accomplish anything for yourself, it is absolutely necessary that you completely believe in yourself.

The truth is that you are never too old, too young, or any of those excuses people are constantly running behind for cover. At any age, life is a beautiful journey. It is full of excitement, adventure and all sorts of wonderful experiences. You cannot allow anyone to tell you that you cannot do this, or you cannot do that. People have to get rid of the old wishbone, and get a little back bone.

If you will just man up and show up, the spirit inside of you will show out. You do not need a wishbone, because the real power lives inside of you, just waiting for you to acknowledge It.

What are you going to do with the power of your gift? In your hands, you hold the keys to the kingdom- through faith you can turn the lock and start living.

Take the first step

Make a decision to do something that will make life better. **All you have to do is start and your mind will begin to activate all the knowledge "know-how" you will need to get the job done, but <u>you have got to get started</u>.**

It is a fact that when we start anything positive that helps to make life better, by our very action, we are saying, "Lord Help Me". **And remember –God truly helps those who help themselves**. A Prime example is the fact that, Yes, it's true that God provides food for the birds- but even they have to leave the nest to go look for it. You cannot accomplish anything by doing nothing. **<u>If you are doing nothing, you can be assured that for your future, you can expect nothing and the result will be nothing</u>.**

<u>You cannot afford to stand still. You have to do something or life will pass you by, this is a fact.</u>

Remember, anything we decide to do is a process and it will take time, **but you got to get started**.

<u>We have to develop awareness that we have things to accomplish in our life.</u>

If we want to reach a goal, we have to get focused, make a plan and set a direction. You have to start by taking small steps. Take one step at a time. Stay on your course. Learn to take the long way home. Taking shortcuts can often lead to failure. Learn to appreciate every step where you are successful with a spirit of gratitude. This will allow the law of attraction to help you achieve even more successful steps in the direction of your goals.

<u>These are the steps needed to get started.</u>

1. Start with yourself, by asking these honest questions.

A. Does it make sense to change from my present condition?
B. Do I believe this is something that I can do?
C. What benefits would I receive, if I do change?
D. How will the change make my life different?

2. Abandon all excuses.

3. Instead of doing nothing, simply get started.

4. Learn to focus and control your thoughts.

5. Learn to be thankful for the small success.

CHAPTER #5

"Faith is taking the first step, even when you don't see the whole staircase"

Martin Luther King. Jr.

Thoughts are powerful.

To begin with, you must understand that all positive change depends on a clear understanding, that our thoughts are the creative force. Thoughts have created our present conditions.   And thoughts will shape our future conditions. **The real business in life is** thinking. Therefore, any man, who can control his thoughts, can control his circumstances. **You must be able to control the thoughts you are entertaining.**   Thoughts create positive and negative conditions in our lives. They send out vibration energy. **This is what Jesus meant when He said in Mark 7:15 "it is what comes out of a man that defiles him".** It also defines him. Jesus understood the law of our being. He understood the creative power we possess. **He understood the power of thoughts, and how they are transformed into words, actions and finally conditions**. But the first point of creation starts with what we think. Therefore, you have to entertain only thoughts that promote life. People should think thoughts that seek a better life for them and others. Thoughts **that do not** seek to harm others are what you should be thinking. What you should be thinking about all the time are positive and constructive thoughts, which help to bring you closer to your goals. Thoughts produce energy. Energy follows thought: **In our thinking, what**

we assume, expect and believe, creates our experiences. By changing our thinking and expectations, we change our experience in every aspect of our lives. We become transformed by the renewing of our minds. **Moreover, in our efforts to change our lives, we should learn to avoid people, and situations, which are counterproductive to our goals. People who seem to enjoy drama, chaos and confrontation, are equally harmful to our cause. You cannot allow them to drop those negative vibes into your spirit.**

Moving forward

In order to move forward, you must make a decision to place a goal before you, and then you must have faith. You have to have faith that God will help you. And you have to believe in yourself. **You have the ability to make your goal a reality. The power is inside of you.** You must understand that faith is the primary ingredient needed to change your present conditions, to achieving your goals, to making your dreams a reality. Everyone you see, who is successful, whether on T.V., at work or where ever, all share this common factor, they all believed they could achieve their goals. It is no different for you; you will have to believe in yourself.

Consider this; most people are walking around on automatic pilot. **They are so stuck in their daily routines, that they rarely consider any other possibilities.** They lack personal ambition. They are not motivated. They live life with even less inspiration. They are travelling on the seas of life, without any real destination. They have not set a course to anywhere. They neglect their right to choose. **They simply go with the flow, and if life has taught us anything, it has taught us that any man or woman, who does not make a** conscious decision to choose and plot a course for their life, will soon find themselves moving towards becoming a victim of circumstances, another statistic of a failed life.

However, this does not have to be the case. You have the power to become the captain of your destiny. You can plot the course.

How is this done?

First, you have to make a conscious decision to choose what you want to be and how you want to live. You are no different than anyone else, who has acquired success in life. However, in order to bring about a lasting change in your life, you will have to get focused on a single idea. Make that idea your personal little project. **Set one goal at a time. Learn to concentrate on one success at a time. Remember – many small goals can amount to one big success.**

One of the greatest mistakes people make is this: they look around, they are unhappy with their present conditions.

They say they want their life to change. They swear that things are going to change, and at that PRESENT MOMENT, they honestly want things to change. Their moment of discomfort fuels their desire. They will tell you and anyone standing long enough to listen, how things are going to change, and you see them a year later, and Nothing Has Changed. Their problem lies in the fact, that their desire is not strong enough. It is not a lasting desire. Consequently, they are not focused on change and nothing changes.

When you get focused on what you want, your desire will be constant. You become determined. It is at that point, that your mind's thinking power begins to work with you in finding a way to reach your goals. Through your strong desire, you begin to activate the power of the gift you possess.

Moreover, to bring about change, you have to know yourself, the real you. You must never lose sight of this supreme fact. Your true nature is three fold, mind, body and spirit. And of the three, your spirit is all knowing. It is a part of God (His Spirit), given to everyone and that includes you. You must learn to trust it. You must nourish it and keep it healthy. A healthy spirit is priceless.

Learn to be Still

In order to move forward, you will have to concentrate with clarity and POWER. Therefore, in your efforts, you will need to find time for a few quiet moments each day. Some people call it going into "silence", and "some call it meditation". This is the process where we shut the world and all of its noises out. This is where we turn our thoughts within, to feel our true selves. This is similar to meditation, except for the fact that you should be able to just sit quietly almost anywhere.

The idea is to find a spot where you will not be disturbed. Next, simply relax, and shut the world out.

It is here, that we learn to control, and direct our thoughts, for the purpose of accomplishing our goals. I cannot over emphasize the importance of learning to be still. Silence is truly golden. It's important to learn to just be still.

We live in a world that specializes in distractions.

Our world is one in which we are constantly bombarded with sounds from every direction. Whether it is the sound of traffic, sirens, people who are loud or whatever, there is noise and distractions in every direction. With distractions every minute of the day, how can you expect to get focused on anything? You cannot. Therefore, you must learn to take a few minutes out of your busy day to just be still.

There is a beautiful verse in the bible, Psalms 46:10 that says, "Be still and know that I am God" and yet, another in Exodus 14:13 that says, "Stand still and see the salvation of the Lord." When we are still, we gain inner peace. We gain confidence. It is this confidence through inner peace, that we know with assurance that we do not have to be anxious about realizing our goals and dreams because we are assured that they are becoming a reality. This is why in the bible Philippians 4-6, we are instructed to "Be anxious for nothing.... But with thanksgiving, let our request be known to God". And this is because we are partners with the only real power in the entire universe.

Remember – whenever you think desire into the universe, you should expect your thought efforts along with your actions to become a reality.

They always have and they always will, the only difference is that, **now you are learning how to intelligently bring the things into your life that you really want.**

Once you have made a conscious choice to bring change into your life, you must begin to act the part. If your goal is to be successful, then start acting the part of a successful person.

You now have the knowledge of the truth. You already know that the power of your thinking has set a force in motion that cannot fail.

You have to believe and know that your desire is on the way. Learn to speak of your goal as an already existing fact. **Speak of it, as though it is.** Also, you have to provide the proper nourishment for your desire. When you believe and keep the faith, you are nourishing your desire. **Jesus says in Mark 11:24" Therefore I tell you, whatever you ask in prayer, you should believe that you have it and you shall". His advice was to believe and not doubt, simply believe.**

Therefore; you must abandon any thoughts of doubt or fear. Doubts and fears choke and destroy the positive energy you have set in motion. Each thought carry with it its own energy. Positive or negative you are the creator. **Only you can choose your thoughts.** This is why belief and faith are important. **It does not matter what the situation looks like to your eyes. In Proverbs 3-5, we are instructed to "Trust in the Lord with all of your heart and lean not to your own understanding"** When you trust God, you must abandon thoughts of "what if this happens, or if that doesn't happen". Thoughts like those are doubt and fear in disguise. They only serve to destroy your faith and belief. **You cannot afford to entertain thoughts of doubt and fear, the price is too high, you must keep your faith. You have to know and believe with confidence that you are making a real change in your life.**

You have to stay your course, believe it; know it, and start to look for the signs that give you assurance that you are on the right track. They are there. **Also, remember that there is always a space of time between planting seeds,**

growing and the actual harvest. You must practice faith with patience.

A great act of faith occurs when you are able to thank God that He has given you your desires, even though they are not yet seen. Your action of thanking Him in advance shows confidence that you know that your desires are on the way and by doing this, you are demonstrating your faith and belief. The two go hand and hand. You cannot have one, without the other.

If you have faith, then it serves to reason that you also believe. It is by virtue of the law of Cause and Effect, that our actions allow law to work for us, making our desires a reality.

These are the steps needed to move forward in faith:

1. You have to make a decision about what you want out of life.

2. Make goals, and be determined to achieving them.

3. You have to believe in yourself, and in your ability to change your life.

4. With a constant thought, you must concentrate only on the things you want.

5. Visualize success. Learn to feel the joy of your success.

6. You will have to nourish your desire with faith in God and by thanking Him in advance

7. You must learn to Be Still and meditate.

CHAPTER #6

"It is not enough to have a good mind; the main thing is to use it well"

Rene Descartes

What Is The Real Secret?

Mind is the secret, which is no secret at all. Although it is no secret, there are a few fundamental truths which must be fully grasped and understood, that will help you use the power you possess positively and effectively. Our first area of concern has to do with the fact that, man has two minds in one. The first mind is, **the conscious mind**. We use our conscious mind when we speak, see, touch, taste and smell. It is our conscious mind that allows us to be aware of this present moment. It is through the conscious mind that we are able to reason between right and wrong, what truth is, and what a lie is. It understands only the present moment. That is why it is called the conscious mind. It is aware of the here and now.

The second mind is called, **the subconscious mind.** This mind operates all of our involuntary body functions, such as the beating of our heart, the disposal of waste, blood circulation, and body repair work. The subconscious mind has eternal wisdom. Its wisdom springs from the Creator.

The conscious mind and subconscious mind are two distinct minds. They serve different functions. And although they serve different functions, it is a fact that the subconscious mind serves the conscious mind.   The fact that it is called sub-conscious mind suggest, that it is under something, namely in this case, conscious mind. This is how it works. It is the nature of the conscious mind to reason. It determines whether a situation makes sense or not. When the conscious mind determines that information is correct, it sends this information to the subconscious mind. The subconscious mind cannot reason. It cannot determine the truth from a lie. Whatever, the conscious mind makes sense of, it sends to the subconscious mind. The subconscious mind can only react to information received from the conscious mind. The subconscious mind is a servant of the conscious mind, and as such, it does what it is told. It obeys.

This is why it is often difficult for people to change their lives. As long as it makes sense to their conscious mind, they will continue in the same direction.   When it no longer makes sense to the conscious mind, it is at that point, change will begin to take place.

Unlike the conscious mind, the subconscious mind has no say in the matter of deciding.   The conscious mind decides what Is and what Is Not. It then passes the information on to the subconscious mind.

The subconscious mind acts as a cosmic soil, by (receiving) the information passed to it, and thereby begins to make the information a reality. It is through a conscious constructive and creative thought pattern, fueled by wisdom, understanding and knowledge, that we bring prosperity and happiness into our lives.

And although the conscious and subconscious minds are active forces in promoting success, before we can begin to think prosperity into our lives from an intelligent prospective, we have to acknowledge the great mind, which is called **the universal mind**. Some simply call it intelligent spirit. <u>I call it God.</u> Whatever you decide to call it is a matter of personal opinion or choice. However, the fact remains that it exists. In a sense, we may look at the subconscious mind as the soul of man. From our conscious mind, we choose our thoughts. Afterwards, they are planted into the subconscious mind. The subconscious mind is our direct connection to universal mind. It is our direct line to the power and wisdom of God. Therefore, it is through the subconscious mind, that we have the ability to accomplish any goal set before us. It is through our conscious thinking that our subconscious mind receives information. Once the subconscious mind receives it, it passes the information on into universal mind.

The universal mind makes our thoughts a reality. This is why it is important to think wholesome clean thoughts. You cannot entertain negative non-productive thoughts, and expect success, good health and prosperity. Corrupt thinking prevents the spiritual flow we otherwise would receive. **Right thinking is what we need at every turn in our lives**.

In further analysis, we can go a step farther, and view the relationship between **conscious, subconscious, and universal mind like this**: our conscious mind is our connection between the external world, and the subconscious mind. Accordingly, the subconscious mind is our connection between conscious and universal mind. The relationship is one described in the following example:

External World—Conscious mind----Subconscious mind—Universal mind.

External world (things going on around you)

Conscious mind (your present moment awareness)

Subconscious mind (your key to moving spirit)

Universal mind (The source of all power)

Make no mistake; The Universal mind is all knowing, all present, and all powerful.

By understanding the working of our mind, we get a better understanding that we can tap into   universal divine spirit. The only way to intelligently use the power we have inside, is through our conscious thinking, which sends messages to our subconscious and ultimately, to the universal mind, the true seat of authority. When we know this, it only serves to reason that we have to make a conscious effort to send the right messages to the subconscious mind. Our mind is part of the universal spirit mind and since it is, on the one hand, it can meet our needs, and make our dreams come true; on the other hand, by thinking negative non productive ill thoughts, it can create a state of living hell, especially when we entertain thoughts which are negative and unwholesome. It can also guard and protect us from harm of any kind. It is through consistent application of right thinking, that it works.

I am reminded of a story I heard as a child, and never forgot it. As the story went, there was a woman who had to be admitted to the hospital in a distant southern town due to a chronic case of tuberculosis. Now this woman had three children at the time, and these children were left in the care of a friend of the family. What the ailing woman did not know, was that while she was away sick in the hospital, her children were being mistreated. One day, one of her children wrote her a letter, explaining that they were being ill treated. And as a result, the ailing woman began to pray, asking God to heal her body so that she would be able to return home. Shortly after beginning her constant prayer, this woman claimed that the Lord had spoken to her, and assured her that she would be leaving the hospital in the month of March. In her excitement, the woman shared this information with other patients on her ward. It was February at the time. Now, when the first week of March arrived, everyone on the ward came around with the comment, "I thought you were going home in March". The woman told me that this joking continued for about two weeks into March. At that point, she became irritated by the comments and said firmly, "Listen, March carries thirty one days, and I am going home this month". During this time, she continued in her prayer and belief that she would be going home in March. The day was now March 30th, and the woman was up early this particular morning, praying. It was nearing the time for the night nurse to be relieved by the morning nurse. When the morning nurse arrived, she asked the night nurse, "How do you feel this morning"? The reply was, "I feel pretty good" and with that, the morning nurse continued with, "well you should feel good, because you have a release from your floor today", "my floor, she responded", "yes! Mrs. M is being released today". Mrs. M heard those words with distinct clarity. Upon hearing those words, she let out a loud shout of joy. Thank you Lord, Thank you. In fact, she shouted so loud that she woke up the entire ward. Suddenly, all of the doubting Thomas's had to take a back seat. She had many visits from patients on that day, anxious to talk to her as she packed in preparation to go home. Consider this; the woman told me, the reason why people did not believe she would leave the hospital in March was because, usually, patients were not released from the second floor. They were only released from the first floor and that would be after the approval from the doctors stating that the tuberculosis was in remission. The fact that this woman was released from the second floor could have been considered a miracle and it in fact was a miracle. I truly believe that it was because of her strong desire to return home to be with her children, the power of the gift inside of her began to make her desires a reality.   She believed in the power of God to get her home and she never doubted it. She had a conscious belief and this was fed into the subconscious mind. It orchestrated the events which would make her desire a reality.

As with her, you too possess the power to make your desires come true. She used her divine birth right and so can you. **When we accept our birth right as creators, we will be able to face any situation as another opportunity to prove that the power inside of us through our faith is real.**

Remember, thoughts are powerful. "**Thoughts produce a force of energy that is creative.**

Through our thinking, we can affect any situation. There is no limit. The only limit is that which the person places on himself.   You have to stop doubting your ability**. Instead, visualize how you want things to be. See it in your mind. Say out loud – "I already have the things I need". "My desires are here already". They are a reality.** Even if you cannot see them, you must believe that they exist.

Remember, all of your conscious thinking and reasoning registers in your subconscious mind, which sends the message to universal mind.

It is in the realization of the power inside of you, that you are made free of the worldly ball and chain. Try

it and learn to trust it. It cannot fail. Every time you make a positive statement about your well being; your success and your happiness, you impress the thought into your subconscious mind, and since the subconscious mind does not reason, but only reacts –it therefore stand to reason that the very moment you convince the subconscious mind that your statements are true – it is at that same moment **universal mind** will make it true. This is what the writer Paul meant in the bible **Ephesians 3-20** when he said, "**and now unto Him who is able to do exceeding abundantly above all that we ask or think ACCORDING to the power that works in us.**" **The key is within us. We have to know with confidence. This is what the bible means when it says "greater is he that is in me, than he that is in the world". They are talking about the God force that we possess inside, which is the power of the gift.**

In light of this fact, we have to get rid of any doubt. The master advice was, "Believe that ye receive it, and ye shall have it". Matthew 21:22 Believe – not doubt – simply believe with all your heart.

There is no room to doubt ourselves. **We must not doubt our spiritual ability.** We are made in the image of the one true God.

Doubting for us is like Kryptonite to Superman. Doubt takes away our positive energy; it kills our enthusiasm, and robs us of success. We doubt, because we cannot see how our needs and desires can come to us. **We fail to see that we are not alone, and as a result of this, we put a limit on God. How can this be? Just look around, can't you see that God is a NO LIMIT GOD. Those people, who have acquired success and happiness in their lives, know that, He is the author of Unlimited Potential and Infinite Possibilities.**

And when I speak of unlimited potential and infinite possibilities, I am talking about you. However, nothing will work for you, until you know in your heart that it is real.

In the book of Malachi, our Creator says "Prove me now herewith saidth the Lord of Hosts; if I will not open the windows of heaven and pour you out a blessing that there shall not be room enough to receive it." Basically He is saying "If you don't believe, then put Me to the test" Prove me now herewith means, test Me now along with your faith. Also, if you will notice, He said pour out a blessing, not send down a blessing. If you know anything about pouring, it suggests a constant flow. He is talking about a flow, which once it is started, will continue, so long as we engage in constructive thoughts, which promote life for ourselves and others.

You are here to experience life and to have an abundant life at that. It is high time that you stop short changing yourself. The only real requirement is that **YOU MUST CHOOSE** – there is no other way. **To expect less is to get less. You are creating your own reality**.

I would like for you to take a minute right now, and think about this: the all powerful, all knowing, eternal Creator is the same power that works in you. What do you think Jesus meant when He said in John 10-34 "Is it not written in your law that you are gods" Look it up, it is there. And to the extent that you know this, will you be able to bring about the changes in your life that you desire. This is the Power of the Gift from our Creator; we possess the power to bring about positive change, in spite of our circumstances.

This is the real secret of how things work on this planet we call Earth.

Positive change is brought about through the power of your mind, your divine nature. And exactly what does that mean? Well, it means that positive thoughts put us in a position to use the power we have inside to realize our dreams and make joy and happiness a lasting reality. Whereas, all negative thoughts block our inspirational energy flow

Also, we must never judge our brothers and sisters, the job of JUDGE is already taken, and neither you nor I hold the position.

We have to respect, accept and pray for our brothers and sisters. In order to change our lives for the better, we have to entertain only those thoughts that build. Not thoughts that build only for us, but for others as well. We must learn to help where ever we can.

Learn to encourage, motivate and inspire. And when we inspire and motivate, the law of Cause and Effect will bring the same back to us. How can we lose? We cannot.

Remember – we use the invisible spirit substance to build ourselves physically, mentally and spiritually. And it is also used to create our conditions and environment. **In order to create, you must first give mentally. And what you give depends on what you are on the inside. And what you are on the inside depends on what you think. "As a man thinketh in his heart, so is he". The results we get are a direct reflection of who we are on the inside.**

Also – another aspect of the secret, is Love. Love is the strongest vibration in the universe. Love is everything. It is the real key to life, and it is the power of love that moves the world. When all is said and done, love is the only thing that will matter. And since we come from love, it is man's inherent nature to receive, and give love. The concept of love is: loving ourselves and others, as they are, without judgment or reservation. Love is expressed by treating people with awareness that there is a part of God in every person. When we love without condition or restraint, we connect with our god-self. When we operate in the spirit of love, we instinctively say the right things at the right time.. Life is more joyous and agreeable. Everything seems to flow with ease when we live in unconditional love. Those men and women who walked on the planet at some past time and left their mark on the world, were not only seeking fame and fortune, they also loved humanity. They had a conscious knowledge of who they were. They knew better than anyone else, the gifts which were placed in them and they were determined not to let them go to waste. They made a decision to do something that would make the world a better place. They understood that by using their talents in the best possible way, they were showing their love for God. They learned to look for the best in people. It was through their personal love for what they were doing and their love for humanity that they were able to hold on, keep the faith and continued without weakening. **To achieve anything, you have to be strongly committed. You have to be able to hold on to your belief with a single purpose, accomplishing your goals and making your dreams a reality.**

Answer these questions: what makes one person successful and another fail? Is it not their actions? And where do our actions come from? Is it not true that our actions are the result of our thinking? If you believe this is true, then at what point are you going to change your thinking so that your life will change. <u>If not now, then when?</u> Now is the acceptable time. There is no time like the present. Time is valuable; it is what life is made of. And time my friend, waits for no one.

The secret to success:

1. Understand that thoughts are powerful.

2. Learn how the mind works spiritually.

3. Understand that human potential is infinite.

4. Understand that the power is inside of you.

5. Understand that you must be committed to your goals.

6. Understand that time waits for no one.

CHAPTER # 7

"Nothing great will ever be achieved without great men, and men are great only if they are determined to be so"

Charles de Gaulle

<u>How strong do I have to be?</u>

It's amazing the way life just goes on, and as long as we are seeking answers with patience, they will come. When I reached this chapter – I began to question myself with that very thought – How strong do I have to be? Consequently, I thought, and I thought, about how I should start this chapter. It was not through my thinking that my question was answered, but through life. As you will clearly remember, in previous chapters, I stated emphatically that we should trust our own thinking and individuality. Even more so, we should trust our Inner Spirit – **The Creator.** Now, when I refer to trusting the Creator, I am talking about having the ability to move on faith. Surprisingly, just before I began to write this chapter – I received a letter in the mail from the Department of Veterans Affairs. The letter stated in short, that there was **<u>an outstanding warrant, out for my arrest, since 2007.</u>**

What a slap in the face that was! That meant that, I would not be eligible for benefits, until such time as the warrant was satisfied. Now, after receiving this letter, and reading it, I started to ask myself, the question – How strong do I have to be? To be perfectly honest with you, when I received the letter, although I tried to maintain my composure, I was visibly shaken and disappointed, because **a:** even though I was sure that there was no active warrant for me, I began to second guess myself, and **b:** I was discouraged and disappointed in the fact of knowing that my benefits would be delayed even longer, due to this mix-up. Accordingly when I stood back, and took an honest look at the matter I could not help but to relate my present situation to this chapter How strong do you have to be, and as these events unfolded, through it all, I could see the Creator at work, teaching me a lesson in strength.

To sum it up – when I went to the court house to get the matter settled, I was immediately met by a young lady who had a very nonchalant attitude. She told me that I had to wait for someone else – who would handle my case and that, that person would not arrive until 9:00am, at that time it was about 8:15 am. This would mean that I would have to wait 45 minutes before I was seen. At that point, I resolved that, I would be patient and handle my business. I was not about to be discouraged because, I didn't have a choice in the matter. My only option was to stay and take care of business.

I didn't want to risk the chance of an error in the computer being the cause of my arrest. Heaven forbid. At this point, I would like to remind you of the Apostle Paul's words when he said that the spirit flows through all and is in all**. So knowing this, it also follows that the spirit can pull help for us from the four corners of the earth if that's what's needed at the time.**

And, in a manner of speaking, that's just what happened. To my surprise the next woman to come into the office was an old friend of mine whom I had not seen in years. To my amazement, when I explained what had happened, she was more than anxious to help me resolve my situation.

Not only did she resolve the computer error with the warrant, she also called another office and had them give me a written document stating that the matter was closed.

I shared this story with you to bring out a few points –first to be strong, we have **to TRUST OUR CREATOR – OUR SOURCE with everything in our lives.** Proverbs 3-5 says: "**Trust in the Lord with all of your heart, lean not to your own understanding".** Never mind the way things look to your eyes. You must believe and know that you are in the care of a loving Creator.

If you will recall, I stated that upon receipt of the letter, I was visibly shaken and disappointed. I learned from that little episode that in order to be strong, we must be able to put things in their proper perspective.

<u>Proper perspective for me is the fact that I am in the care of a loving Creator, and I should never lose sight of that fact. For me to lose sight of that is to give in to the illusions of life, this in turn will lower my inspiration, expectation and positive energy.</u>

And although I sometimes forget it, it has been my experience that usually things are never as bad as they seem. How could I have known that the person to assist me on that day would be a friend from my past? And no matter what the situation looked like to me, <u>EVERYTHING </u>was alright, just as it should have been at that very moment. Now taking that into consideration, I have come to the conclusion that <u>in order to be</u> <u>strong, </u>you have to know and stand on truth. In other words, before you can move from one point in your life to another, you have to know the truth about who you are and your relationship with God. People could read this until "the cows come home" but this is something that has to be experienced. Only then will you be able to stand in the face of any seemingly – adverse condition. No matter what comes, you will be able to stand because you not only know the truth, but more importantly, you live truth.

Truth makes us free from fear and doubt. **It is truth that makes us strong. When you stand on truth, it is hard to be moved. You cannot knock a man or woman down standing on truth. In the words of Martin Luther King Jr," Truth crushed to Earth shall rise again".** This is why it is important that we seek wisdom and understanding, so that we may know the truth about life.

 Once we have come into the knowledge of the truth, we have a moral obligation to teach our youth. They must not be neglected.

Tragically, I see many of our youth doing the same things, day in and day out. Whether it's selling drugs, gang banging or just hanging around doing nothing, it is all non-productive. What they must be taught is that man grows from his experiences. How can they grow with the same old experiences? They cannot. They only create a self imposed prison operating on the law of "what goes around comes around". **If you are doing the same thing, you will get the same thing. You have to do something different. It's called change**. Ironically, if they could only find a reason to change, the transition would be easier than they may expect. It is a fact that spirit is ever expanding. The greatest secret of life is that God sends man to earth that he may grow spiritually. He also places inside of man a creative nature that can be used to help him at every turn in his life. Outside of the fact that spirit is inside of man, there is also spiritual energy all around us.

However, to activate the power of the spirit, we have to direct it from our inner world which is the soul of man. We have to go into our secret closet, close the door, and then connect to the only power in the universe, which can change our present condition. In support of this secret, during my college years, I took a course called great philosophers, and on one occasion, the professor shared an interesting story with us. He said that it had come down from Greek Mythology. In this story, he explained that three gods got together with the goal of hiding the key to man's happiness. One god said, "I think we should hide the key to man's happiness on the highest mountain top on earth". Another said, "No because man is adventurous and he will scale the mountain top and find the key". Another said "lets hide the key in the depths of the ocean" to the reply from another that that was a bad idea, because man is an explorer and would one day explore the ocean depths and locate the key. They thought and thought and finally the last god said "I know where we will hide the key to man's happiness, we will place the key to man's happiness right inside of him AND HE WILL NEVER THINK TO LOOK THERE". It will be right under his nose. And although this is just a myth, it serves to bring out a very good point. It is a fact that most people are constantly looking outside of themselves to find joy, happiness and peace. When in reality you can never have peace and happiness, unless it is first found within yourself.

Another equally important component in answering the question – how strong do I have to be is the concept of being you. In order to be strong, you must possess the courage to be yourself. I cannot over emphasize this point. Please excuse the repetition. **But, you have to be rigorously honest about who you are, and what you feel**. You cannot just go with the flow. Individuality is having the ability to be around others, and maintain your own identity.

You cannot expect to receive clear, strong, guidance and inspiration from your Source, when you are living a lie by not being yourself. There is nothing weak about the universe.

And know it or not, you are a part of this great universe. <u>We come from strength</u>. We are made in the image of GOD. And there is <u>NOTHING ABOUT GOD THAT IS WEAK.</u> **<u>Our challenge is to accept our birth right. We are made in the image of the greatest power in eternity.</u>**

We have to stand up and claim the very strength that we are a part of. We have to know that our strength lies in our full confidence in God, and in the power of His Might. Knowing that when we identify and pursue our purpose in life full force, this very desire will generate all the strength and inspiration we need to accomplish any goal placed before us. **<u>You see, we are striving to grow into the knowledge of the truth that GOD really does have our back</u>**. He has created us. He means us no harm, only goodness. **I am encouraging you to be strong, be brave, be confident and you will triumph. And what is triumph, but TRI with a little UMPH. Remember, the sky really is the limit – So shoot for the moon, and even if you miss the moon – who knows, you just might hit a star.**

<u>This is what you need to be strong.</u>

1. You have to know, and accept the truth about life.

2. You have to know who you are, and your relationship with God.

3. You have to be able to find strength by trusting God.

4. You have to follow spiritual laws.

5. You must learn to be confident in God and in the power of His might.

CHAPTER # 8

We are body, mind and spirit, created to experience life. This being true – Spirituality is the lessons that help us build character, and strengthen our inner-self."

Inspired Author

<u>Spirituality</u>

The outward individual is a very limited part of who we really are. And because we walk in darkness, we are ignorant of our true selves. As a result of not knowing our true identity, we use what we have, our possessions, what we do in the world or how we are viewed by others to give us a false sense of identity. We are constantly trying to allow these external things to define who we are. Moreover, since the world on which our identity is based, is constantly changing, this false sense of identity is always under attack. It is a result of our attempts to maintain this false sense of identity, which is responsible for much of our self-centered and prideful behavior. People have also been known to get physically confrontational when their false identity is challenged. This is because their identity is based on a lie, thus they are emotionally unstable, and fearful of being unmasked.

It is a fact that whenever we seek to derive our identity from any outside source – we are going in the wrong direction. We are building our houses on sand as oppose to a solid rock of truth. And when a house is built on sand – any storm will shake its foundation. Why do you think so many individuals from the great stock crash of 1929 jumped out of windows, or put pistols in their mouths? It was because their identities were centered on their status and financial possessions. When their possessions left, they did too.

It is a fact that behind our surface identity is a deeper identity, our "true self" – the spirit of man which is eternal. It is when we discover this true sense of identity, that we are freed from many of the fearful illusions of life. It is only when we recognize our inner self, and nourish it with right thinking and positive actions, do we discover the meaning of inner peace.

We develop a confidence that does not depend upon events, possessions, titles or circumstances in the world around us. As a result of this inner confidence, we become less self-centered. It becomes, no longer, all about us. We become more willing to help others. We become less dependent on the approval and recognition of others. We no longer feel that it's important to get as many possessions as we can collect. <u>This inner confidence results in becoming happier, healthier and loving people.</u>

<u>This is spirituality.</u>

Accordingly, it is through spirituality that we reach a state where we are connected to GOD, and each other. It is that part of us that honestly expresses who we are, and what we are feeling. Therefore, in order for us to perform to our highest potential we must be honest about life. We have to be honest about who we are and our present condition. When we are honest, we are nourishing our spirit. If we are going to have the life we are dreaming of, it is only through our rigorous honesty that we are open to the changes we will need to make our dreams a reality.

And although we are fully aware of our need for material gain, we cannot just focus on the materialistic and altogether neglect the spiritual. When we learn to be spiritual beings, we will have the things we need to bring peace and prosperity in our lives. Moreover, as it relates to being spiritual, people have to be led away from the misconception that to be spiritual, you have to look and sound like a saint. This is not the case.

We are all human. And as such, we are subject to trial and error. All the saints are in Heaven.

Being spiritual is not difficult. It is actually one of the natural states of man. You can experience being spiritual when you are listening to inspirational music, or when you are doing something that is promoting and enhancing life. Also, after a good physical workout session, or after a relaxing shower when you are just laying still and enjoying the present moment.

These things are spiritual because you are enjoying them in innocence. You are not thinking or wishing malice to anyone. You are simply enjoying the moment. Spiritual moments occur when you are not trying so hard to be..., you just are.

It is in these moments that your inner spirit is touched. These actions create feelings of contentment and carefree joy, which connects you spiritually to the Creator. Even the moment you are presently enjoying, connects you to GOD.

You can also experience spiritual moments when you connect with nature. Examples would be walking along the beach, and viewing the ocean. Moreover, you experience a spiritual connection when you work with others for a common cause. Spirituality happens, when you are playing on a sports team, or anything that involves teamwork, or helping others.

As I stated in earlier chapters, we are vibrational creatures. It is when we are in tune with GOD, each other and ourselves, that we are being spiritual. It is through spirituality that the inner man is made strong and thereby ready, willing and able to assist us in accomplishing any desire or goal we wish to realize.

"I will call this higher part of the universe by the name of God. We and God have business with each other; and in opening ourselves to His influence our deepest destiny is fulfilled".

William James

<u>Conclusion</u>

There is no doubt that spirituality is needed in our lives if we are going to enjoy the life we are dreaming of. When we are able to recognize, appreciate and effectively use the power of the gift we possess inside, our lives will be better and our suffering will lessen. As I mentioned in the chapter "spirituality", to be spiritual does not mean that we have to walk around acting like a saint or the pope. When I think of living a spiritual life, I envision living a life that is inspirational or in other words, a life that is inspired by spirit.

I acquaint the word inspire with, being in-spirit. Therefore, when we begin to live a life of inspiration, we are in fact living in spirit.

We are spiritual beings and as such, we perform better, when we are in our own element. That element is the spiritual flow of life, which has the power to rejuvenate and inspire us. Spirit has a universal beat of its own. It is the heart beat of life, and it is always developing. It is eternally present and patient. It only awaits our recognition of it to help us achieve our goals. When we allow spirit to flow through us by right thinking, we become so transformed that our friends will hardly recognize us. And since Spirit is all around us; we are always in a position to be inspired. Furthermore, when we are consciously receptive to its positive energy through positive thinking, we find ourselves doing things, we never imagined possible. Many times we amaze ourselves. We have to be aware of the fact that, when spirit is involved, the entire equation will change.

Often, I have wondered, how is it that the musicians and artist of the world do the magnificent work that they do. I did not understand how they possessed the ability to achieve greatness. Now after coming to understand the power of the spirit, I now know that, they are inspired by spirit.

As with them, we too, can be certain that as long as we are thinking positive thoughts, we can always count on the power of spirit to help us. **Spirit is not a respecter of persons.** It does not matter who you are, so long as you are abiding by the laws of spirit, It will assist you in achieving your goals.

People, who have come to the knowledge of the truth, understand that to be inspired in life, you must be in tune with spirit. The vibrations of spirit are confidence, kindness, patience, and unconditional love. When we are doing things that make life better for others, we are in tune with the spirit of the universe.

It is when we seek first, the kingdom of heaven by doing work inspired by spirit that we shall come into a complete understanding that, all other things shall be added unto us.

Spirit is all knowing, all powerful, all present and ever willing to help us. The only limit that spirit has is that it has to work through us. As it relates to the life of man, spirit of itself will do nothing for him without a word or thought. In this lies the confirmation that "life and death is in the power of the tongue," And "as a man thinketh in his heart, so is he". We must therefore, come to understand that in order to activate spirit, we must think thoughts or speak words, which are positive and life giving. Man is no more or no less than he thinks himself to be.

In operating within the law of spirit, **it is through experience that we gain confidence**. In our life experience, we know that if we had a garden and wanted tomatoes, we would have to plant tomato seeds. We would not plant melon seeds and expect to receive a harvest of tomatoes. This is the same way the law of the spirit works through our thoughts. If we are looking to live a life of prosperity and success, we will have to entertain thoughts of wealth and achievement, which the law of attraction will act upon to make our thoughts a reality. And this can only be accomplished by using the power of our minds.

When we decide to make spirit our partner, success is assured. Do you think by any small stretch of the imagination, that spirit is not aware that you have partnered your efforts with it? It knows. Spirit also knows how to pay us for our labors. It knows what our just reward should be. Is it not written, "For eyes have not seen, nor have ears heard nor have entered into the heart of man, the things that God has prepared for those who love Him". And when we decide to take up our cause for the good of mankind, we do not have to worry about having our needs meet. And that's because, **we know who we are, and we have faith in Him, whom we trust.**

The greatness of God is not experiencing a recession, or depression anywhere. Everything He does, He does in a big way. <u>And when we decide to partner with Him, we are moving towards bigger and better things</u>. The more we are determined to leave our mark on the planet by doing work for the good of mankind, the more inspiration we shall receive to accomplish our task. Accordingly, as our minds move beyond the limits of human ability, it is at that point that, all we ask or think spirit will provide for us, **<u>"according to the power that works in us"</u>.**

Man exists, that through him the spirit of God may be expressed. Thus, we can look on the existence of mankind as that of, many vessels, designed for specific purposes. It is through the laws of the spirit, that we are able to be effective in our daily task. And since the laws of the spirit are not God Himself, but His laws, we should view them like any other law of nature. We should view the law as a servant to man. As long as we are using them in a positive, productive manner, we shall prosper. However, when we use the law in a destructive manner, It becomes a chastiser of man. We should understand that, we will reap the efforts of our labor. <u>Galatians 6-7 says "Be ye not deceived, God will not be mocked, and whatever a man sows that shall he reap" In this one scripture, we receive confirmation and wisdom. Basically, it is saying that we are bound by spiritual law and can no more escape it, than to escape the effects of gravity, while walking on earth.</u>

Today can truly be a new beginning. After coming into the knowledge of truth, we now know that, we need not suffer any longer. We have a better understanding that we have been our own worst enemy all along. And our circumstances were actually created by us.

With this knowledge, we now understand the concept of being made in the image of God and the power that comes with it.

And, although man has stumbled in darkness for what seems to be an eternity, it is through understanding the power we possess inside and intelligently using it, that we accept our inheritance as sons and daughters of God. It is on that day, that we will understand the true meaning of "Our Father which art in heaven". It is at that point, that we shall be able to take our rightful place in this wonderful universe; this will be the day when we members of the human race will truly know that Thy Kingdom has come.

Spiritual Laws

SPIRITUAL LAWS

Spiritual laws are the laws of our being. When we function within the laws of the spirit, we are able to accomplish those goals placed before us. Our inner spirit, is governed by spiritual laws. Many times individuals encounter negative situations in their lives simply because they are not consciously aware, that they are breaking spiritual laws. Ignorance of the law is no excuse. Spiritual laws operate the same way that physical laws work. For example, if you were driving, and there was a stop sign you didn't see, and you caused an accident by not obeying the traffic sign, the police officer would not take into consideration the fact that you didn't see the light. The fact would be that you broke the law, and caused damage. You would have to pay for the consequences of your actions. The officer would probably say, although you didn't see the light, non- the –less, you broke the law, and your excuse would be just that, an excuse. And so it is with spiritual laws, ignorance of their existence is no excuse. **They are in effect whether you are aware of them or not. Law is law.**

 Below, I have assembled a series of spiritual laws which work in accordance with our thinking and actions. These are many of the principles which I have incorporated into my own life, and because I make a conscious effort to observe and practice them, they are serving me well. I hope that you too, will find them as valuable as I have and will therefore refer to them often.

THE LAW OF ABUNDANCE

By visualizing abundance in our lives, we draw this energy of success into our reality.

Abundance does not mean you have to have a lot of money. It suggests a sense of well being in all areas of our lives. There is success in spirituality, relationships, finances, health and so on. When we create abundance, we should do the best possible job we can, to create the highest standard in whatever area we are concentrating in at that particular moment.

THE LAW OF CHALLENGE

We have the right to ask of another, his or her intent, identity, and whatever information we feel we require, when dealing with people. Always follow your inner guide (instincts).

THE LAW OF FAITH

The Law of Faith is founded upon the recognition that the truth lives inside of us. We know more than we have read, heard, or studied. We know more, because we are a part of the Creator. We have a direct link to universal wisdom. **We only have to look within, then listen, discern, and finally trust. We need to develop more trust in our own deepest intuition and wisdom as the final source of our decisions.**

THE LAW OF ACCEPTANCE

This law involves acceptance of the present moment. We learn to live in the here and now. We learn to accept ourselves, others and current circumstances as they are. It requires that we learn to appreciate the moment by making constructive use of our time. **Those situations which seem to be problems become opportunities to prevail through inner strength and guidance.** Everything serves our highest good if we make good use of it. The essence of this law is captured in the serenity prayer, **"God grant me the serenity, to accept the things I cannot change, the courage to change the things I can, and the wisdom to know the difference".**

THE LAW OF FORGIVENESS

This law works with the energy of allowing and seeing all as love, and through forgiving, we learn to rid ourselves of the unnatural feeling of getting even.

The old energy of an eye for an eye keeps the vibrations of a person very low. When we forgive others and release old anger, we invite the law of love and grace into our lives. All good comes from forgiveness. Forgiveness is holiness.

By forgiveness, the universe is held together. Forgiveness is the might of the mighty; forgiveness is quiet of mind. Forgiveness is for your own sense of peace as well.

THE LAW OF FREE WILL

We have the right to choose how we want to live our lives. **However, we must be mindful, that any choice we make brings with it positive or negative consequences, of which we can never escape.** This is our ultimate decision. **No matter what our circumstances are, we have the power to choose our direction.** **We also choose to be under the influence of others or choose to be an example for others**

THE LAW OF GROUP ENDEAVOR

This law defines the multiplying of energy one creates when acting with likeminded individuals for a single purpose. Where the efforts of an individual is single power, the efforts of two or more working together in an endeavor, such as praying or working for a common goal, will increase the energy level tremendously.

THE LAW OF HONESTY

Recognizing, accepting and expressing our true self lies at the heart of honesty. **Only when we are honest with ourselves, can we speak or act honestly with anyone else.** When we let fear stop us from expressing our true feelings and needs, we are being dishonest with ourselves, and it costs us a sense of positive energy and spirit.

THE LAW OF NO JUDGEMENTS

There is only ONE JUDGE, and we are not that ONE. No one has the right to judge another. We are here to help and accept others as they are. Through the law of love, we learn to pray for others.

THE LAW OF ONE

The Lord is ONE. All that is, is His, the earth is His and the fullness thereof. In Him do we live, move and have our being.

THE LAW OF PATIENCE

Patience involves spiritual, mental, physical thought and action. Through it, we learn to know our self, to use faith, and to seek understanding. Patiently we realize that any fault we see in another person is one we have personal knowledge of **from prior experience**. **Patiently we seek true understanding, not just knowledge, as we realize that every soul is totally unique, and will come into the knowledge of truth in its own time.**

THE LAW OF HABITS

Any habit whether we call it good or bad, will be repeated over and over again, unless we break it by doing something different. We really do have the power to change.

Some of our patterns (habits) are rooted in the ways we learned when we were young. We learned to make sense of the world by observing others. Through these observations, we developed bad habits. Many times we reasoned that this was what we needed to do to survive. We were wrong. Today, we understand that we can correct our habits of destructive behavior by doing something different, it is called change.

Inspirational Quotes

INSPIRATIONAL QUOTES

I have compiled these inspirational quotes which are relative to the chapters. I find them to be inspiring and motivating. These authors' words are beautiful, uplifting and encouraging. I pray that you will find them to have the same beauty.

Opportunity stands beside you every moment and one of its favorite disguises is that of obstacles.

Author Unknown

Be the change you want to see in the world.

Mahatma Gandhi

I wouldn't have seen it if I hadn't believed it

Marshall McLuhan

You gotta dance like nobody's watching, dream like you will live forever, live like you're going to die tomorrow, and love like it's never going to hurt.

Meme Grifsters

Just don't give up trying to do what you really want to do. Where there is love and inspiration, I don't think you can go wrong.

Ella Fitzgerald

We have more possibilities available in each moment than we realize.

Thich Nhat Hanh

The most authentic thing about us is our capacity to create, to overcome, To endure, to transform, to love, And to be greater than our suffering.

Ben Okri

Our deepest fear is not that we are inadequate. Our deepest fear is that we are powerful beyond measure. It is our light not our darkness that frightens us.

Marianne Williamson

You yourself, as much as anybody in the entire universe deserve your love and affection.

The Budda

The world we have created is a product of our thinking. It cannot be changed without changing our thinking.

Albert Einstein

I gain strength, courage and confidence by every experience in which I must stop and look fear in the face...   I say to myself, I've lived through this and can take the next thing that comes along .....

We must do the things that we think we cannot do.

Eleanor Roosevelt

It is not necessary to deny another's reality in order to affirm your own.

Anne Wilson Schaef

In the end, nothing we do or say in this lifetime will matter as much as the way we have loved one another.

Daphne Roe Kingman

What if the question is not why am I so infrequently the person I really want to be, but why do I so infrequently want to be the person I really am?

Oriah Mountain Dreamer

You are me and I am you. Isn't it obvious that we "inter-are"?

You cultivate the flower in yourself, so that I will be beautiful. I transform the garbage in myself so that you will not have to suffer.

Thich Nhat Hanh

If I accept the sunshine and warmth, then I must also accept the thunder and lightning

Kahlil Gibran

To be yourself- in a world which is doing its best, night and day, to make you like everybody else means to fight the hardest battle which any human being can fight, and never stop fighting.

E.E. Cummings

Meditation is being happy with you for no reason at all.   You are simply in love with yourself, in love with existence.

Tishan

Our deepest wishes are whispers of our authentic selves. We must learn to respect them. We must learn to listen.

Sarah Ban Breathnach

Too often we underestimate the power of a touch, a smile a kind word, a listening ear.... An honest compliment, or the smallest act of caring.... All of which have the potential to turn a life around.

Leo Buscaglia

My dear children: I rejoice to see you before me today, happy of a sunny and fortunate land. Bear in mind that the wonderful things that you learn in your schools are the work of many generations, produced by enthusiastic effort and infinite labor in every country of the world. All this is put into your hands as your inheritance in order that you may receive it, honor it, and add to it. And one day faithfully hand it on to your children. Thus, we mortals achieve immortality in the permanent things which we create in common. If you always keep that in mind you will find meaning in life and work and acquire the right attitude towards other nations and ages.

Albert Einstein

There are admirable potentialities in every human being. Believe in your strength and your youth. Learn to repeat endlessly to yourself, 'It all depends on me."

Andre Gide

I was always looking outside myself for strength and confidence, but it comes from within. It is there all the time.

Anna Freud

Believe in yourself! Have faith in your abilities!
Without a humble but reasonable confidence in
your own powers you cannot be successful or
happy

Norman Vincent Peale

Every time you don't follow your inner guidance,
you feel a loss of energy, loss of power, a sense of
spiritual deadness.

Shakti Gawain

Don't be too timid and squeamish about your
actions. All life is an experiment. The more
experiments you make the better.

Ralph Waldo Emerson

Self-confidence is the first requisite to great
undertakings.

Samuel Johnson

Strong reasons make strong actions.

William Shakespeare

Right and Truth do not have to prove themselves

Lorraine Darling

BIBLIOGRAPHY

Allen, James T. "As a Man Thinketh" ---1902

Emerson, Ralph Waldo "The Over Soul" Essay---1841

Hammer, Frank L. "Life and Its Mysteries"---1945

Hammer, Frank L."An Eternal Career"---1947

Holmes, Ernest "The Creative Mind"---1923

Holmes, Ernest"The Science of Mind"---1926

Shinn, Florence Scovel "Your Word is Your Wand"---1928

Trine, Ralph Waldo "In Tune with the Infinite"---1910

Troward, Thomas "The Edinburgh Lectures on Mental Science"---1909

Troward, Thomas "The Hidden Power" 1921

Troward, Thomas "The Law and the Word"---1921

Printed in the United States
By Bookmasters